OFF
BALANCE
ON
PURPOSE

Keep leaning forward!

OFF BALANCE ON PURPOSE

EMBRACE UNCERTAINTY AND
CREATE A LIFE YOU LOVE

DAN THURMON

Published by Motivation Works, Inc.
Snellville, Georgia
www.danthurmon.com

Copyright ©2016 Dan Thurmon

Distributed by Motivation Works, Inc.

For ordering information or special discounts for bulk purchases, please contact Motivation Works, Inc. at 2134 North Road, Snellville, GA 30078, (770) 982-2664

Thurmon, Dan.

   Off balance on purpose : embrace uncertainty and create a life you love / Dan Thurmon.—2nd ed.

   ISBN: 978-0-9969731-0-6

1. Self-realization. 2. Self-actualization (Psychology) 3. Conduct of life. 4. Happiness. I. Title.

Part of the Tree Neutral™ program, which offsets the number of trees consumed in the production and printing of this book by taking proactive steps, such as planting trees in direct proportion to the number of trees used: www.treeneutral.com

TreeNeutral™

Printed in the United States of America on acid-free paper

13 14 15 16 17   10 9 8 7 6 5 4

Second Edition

To Sheilia, Eddie, and Maggie, with all my love. Thanks for your unwavering support and inspiration . . . and for helping me stay off balance on purpose.

Contents

Part One

EMBRACING CONTRADICTIONS

1

YOU WILL NEVER ACHIEVE BALANCE—AND SHOULDN'T WANT TO

A BALANCED LIFE. Just reading that phrase likely conjures a sense of longing. And why wouldn't it? As you struggle each day to manage the barrage of forces competing for your time, energy, creativity, input, and attention, it's understandable that you want to find a simpler solution—picture a future moment when you are able to expertly allot your resources, perfect your priorities, and celebrate that everything has finally "evened out."

We all crave balance. After all, countless books, talk show programs, and self-help gurus have told us that balance is the solution to our problems. So, it's completely reasonable for you to believe that finding balance in your life is intriguing, attainable, and desirable. Unfortunately, it's also completely unrealistic.

You will never achieve perfect balance. And neither will I. Frankly, I have given up trying to live my life "on balance." Instead, I'm choosing to live *off balance on purpose*. This path and plan of action, as you will soon discover, provides a liberating and empowering alternative to improve the way we can engage life.

Although unconventional and inconsistent with what you have been told by "experts," the off balance on purpose approach is rooted in truth, consistent with reality, and infinitely more practical than the fantasy of trying to attain some mythical balanced condition. When it comes to balance, you have been sold a bill of goods. It's time to give yourself a break, embrace the life you have, and make adjustments that will allow you to grow in the areas that are crucial to your most important commitments as well as your happiness.

Balance Is Unattainable and Undesirable

We use the word *balance* freely and speak of the undeniable attributes of living balanced lives. But words are charged with meaning, and this word in particular embodies a definition that demands closer inspection. According to Webster's *New World College Dictionary*, balance is "a state of equilibrium or equipoise; equality in amount, weight, value, or importance, as between two things or the parts of a thing."

There's more to the definition, but stop right here and ask yourself, Is this really the condition I am looking for in my life—a state of equilibrium? How about "equality in amount, weight, value, or importance"—does that appeal to me? Before you answer, I'd like you to imagine something. Picture a scale.

After all, if we are to seek equality or equilibrium, we will need to measure it. And what better way than a good old-fashioned scale? You know, the kind you used in your high school science class. On one side, let's portion your devotion to your family, friends, and personal endeavors. Go ahead, scoop out a healthy amount—enough to keep you fulfilled, your significant other placated, your offspring well-adjusted and guided, and your friends reminded that you are still alive and well. But not too much!

Because on the other side of the scale we need to dole out the professional you—a person who is committed to your job, your career path, and your ongoing professional development. After all, you need to make some money if you are going to support your family and the lifestyle you want to

lead. And, in your professional life, the demands are significant, the expectations are increasing, and the competition is relentless. So in order to be a productive member of your team, you'll have to throw yourself against the challenge, committing your energy, time, creative thoughts, and unflagging determination. But not too much!

Maybe this doesn't accurately describe what you would try to balance. Perhaps your scale has your desire to become a published poet on one side and your love of food and shelter on the other. Or your love of spending time with your family on one side and your love of pursuing your creative passions on the other. Or your desire to travel the world on one side and opportunities to begin building your career on the other. Complete the mental picture with your own personal example. Regardless, you want to give both sides—every aspect of your life—adequate energy and attention. Just be careful not to devote too much to either side.

Because if you do, you may tip the scales. And remember, we are striving for that state of equilibrium. We are longing for the moment when the scale levels out and strikes a harmonious state of balance. Right?

Let's say you achieve that moment. Then what? How could you ever possibly maintain it? Is it realistic to think that you can keep your life in a balanced state, where everything is just as important as everything else and where everything gets just as much of your focus and energy as everything else? And, ultimately, would you want that? Of course not! If you were to attempt this impossible feat, you would drive yourself bonkers second-guessing every action, contemplating the weight of each decision, and portioning time according to the clock, each second spent here balanced by a corresponding second spent there.

But again, this is an impossible state to achieve anyway. You don't have unlimited resources to tip the scale this way and that, moment by moment, keeping the magical pointer comfortably on the fine point of happiness. You have what you have. And when commitments you have made demand additional time and effort, you have to deal with that situation using the resources available. The question is how. Do you beat yourself up about it, experiencing constant conflict and forestalling enjoyment of your life until you find a way to achieve balance? Or do you embrace your present reality and find comfort in the fact that you are doing what is necessary to keep moving closer to your broader aspirations?

Life is sticky, and you are in the thick stuff. *Life is not a hypothetical future. It's an undeniable present.* It's happening now. And the way you approach challenging moments has immediate impact on everything you do, everyone you love, every part of who you are, and everything you may become.

Off Balance—Our Natural State of Being

Life is off balance, and that is a good thing. Off balance is the way we grow. It is the way we accomplish goals and good deeds. Off balance is our path to living lives that are significant, full of what we deem to be important and worthwhile. Off balance is also the way you love your family, get closer to God, and improve your physical, mental, and emotional well-being. Each of these aspirations requires a decision and a commitment that takes you, at some particular moment, off balance.

It has often been said that nature is balanced, always in perfect harmony. Somewhere deep in the forest, a mouse leaves its borough on its morning commute to work. After all, it must provide food for its ever-expanding family. When the neighborhood snake eats the mouse, we are told it is merely a beautiful expression of nature's perfection and balance.

Tell that to the mouse. I would maintain that, to both the mouse and the snake, this was not a balanced moment. This was serious, off balance business.

It may be true that all systems seek a balanced state, but the part we don't often hear is that those systems never, ever get there. They are still "seeking"! Balance is something we can observe only over a long period of time. (Isn't it beautiful how the seasons in Chicago represent the full spectrum of weather throughout the year?) But in any given moment, we must deal with the reality of our present, unbalanced circumstances. (Damn, it's freezing in February. Has anyone seen my mittens?)

So, if what we are after is a fulfilling, rewarding, meaningful life, we should first understand that we don't live our lives with a constant long-term perspective. We live one moment at a time. And, from that nonnegotiable point of view, life will never be balanced. Were you to ask ten people today "How's life?" you would likely get an assortment of answers including "busy," "wonderful," "hectic," "fantastic," "insane," or "devastating." Not one person, I bet you, would say "balanced." Moment to moment, we are off balance, experiencing fluctuations through new ideas, new demands, new responsibilities, and new desires—as well as constant changes in our resources.

You can learn to be comfortable and proactive in the midst of this turmoil. In fact, you can even thrive in these circumstances! To do so, you just need to learn to experience life's fullness while keeping your composure. Take all that life has to throw at you, but keep your wits about you and maintain an elevated view of what is happening. I know . . . easier said than done, right? The first step is to accept the idea that we are all, in every moment, off balance. That is natural, normal, and wonderful.

Small Adjustments and Forward Perspective

Some people naturally excel in high-pressure circumstances, when change is erupting all around. Life's challenges, emergencies, surprises, and deadlines bring out the best in them. Other people become paralyzed by change and uncertainty. They shut down and withdraw. The disruption of their diligently defended and perpetually precarious comfort zone is too much for them to handle. So they don't. Maybe you are like the first person I described. Or like the second. What is more likely is that you are somewhere between the two extremes. Regardless of where you are on the "managing change" spectrum, you can learn to manage and even embrace life's beautiful unpredictability.

We marvel at the gymnasts, dancers, yoga practitioners, and circus performers who display amazing feats of balance and make it look effortless. Imagine a tightrope walker suspended high above the ground. The audience watches in breathless anticipation as the funambulist (the actual word for a tightrope walker) maintains perfect balance. Or does she? Take a closer look and you'll see that, in order to stay up on the wire, she is constantly making small, critical adjustments. She lifts her "free leg" as a counterweight, shifts her head and shoulders, raises and lowers her arms, or adjusts her balance pole. There is never a moment when the performer is at rest.

In fact, she is never truly "on balance." She is perpetually off balance: making adjustments that bring her through a point of balance, only to readjust on the other side. Most of these movements are so subtle that they are imperceptible to the audience. She makes it look effortless. But the practitioner knows that there is no such thing as achieving balance. And there is no such thing as standing still. She must keep moving forward if she is to reach the other side. Safely traversing the uncertain and unsteady tight wire is something you work—and at times fight—for, step-by-step and moment-by-moment.

We are all just like the tightrope walker. We pass through the moments of balance, but we cannot stay there because life is fluid. What we can

achieve is awareness that allows us to recognize when we are tumbling in an undesirable direction and a mastery that enables us to make the small but critical adjustments that bring us back toward center. If you wonder, "How can I achieve harmony among all of the aspects of my life?" you are asking a flawed question. Instead, you should ask, "What adjustments must I make to keep from falling off the wire, and how can I keep moving forward toward my goal?"

I have some personal experience with funambulism, as both a performer and an instructor. When new students step onto the rope or cable (depending upon the particular rigging), they almost always begin with the same flawed game plan. They stare downward at the wire to ensure that they have the proper footing. And so they fall. Have you ever attempted to achieve something in life and experienced immediate failure because all of your efforts were based on an uninformed and incorrect approach? If so, then you can relate to the immediate frustration of the student.

So what is the solution to this dilemma? If you have ever closely watched professional tightrope walkers, you may recall that they never look down at their feet or the wire or to either side at their hands (or the balance pole). Rather, they keep their head up and look forward toward the goal— the faraway platform—in front of them.

With this single instruction change, this mere shift in perspective— maintaining an upward and forward focus—I've seen novices find new confidence and achieve the breakthrough that enables them to make the trip across. The placement of each foot is not about visual confirmation. It is accomplished through confident movement, deliberate placement that happens with the toes feeling for and then acquiring the wire, and a well-timed shift of  the weight once the foundation is prepared. It isn't easy. But when the students persist and reach the other side, they've learned some important lessons:

- They were never balanced. They were in constant motion, falling one way, then the other, responding to every influence in the environment (the movement of the wire and the position of their body) as well as the mental obstacles of fears, emotions, and uncertainty. The challenge was really to manage those ever-changing factors and make adjustments that would allow them to continue across the wire.

- When focusing down at their feet or out at their hands (the source of the adjustments), they were incapable of determining which adjustments they needed to make, and they would immediately fall.

- By making a shift in perspective, and after a great deal of determined practice, they were eventually able to accurately assess the situation, control their emotions, feel the movement of the wire, and anticipate what to do next.

- In order to move forward on the wire, they had to step—off balance—in the direction they wanted to go. It was unnerving and difficult. But only then could they follow through with action and make forward progress.

Wire walking, even when undertaken with the right perspective, takes hours of practice. There's nothing "instantaneous" about it. It's not about one simple cure-all; it's about recognizing all the factors that play into the experience and maintaining the right perspective and posture. Life's challenges are like that, particularly when we take on any endeavor that is meaningful.

OVERCOMPENSATIONS AND LASTING CHANGES

When we experience imbalance in our lives, we often overcompensate by throwing ourselves headlong in another direction. We think that it takes bold, dramatic action to create change. Sometimes this is true—we reach moments in our lives when a huge shift in thinking or action is completely necessary. But usually when we find ourselves in that predicament, it is because we missed many previous opportunities to make smaller adjustments that would have prevented, or at least softened, the crisis. Often an attempt to overdo it, providing too much force in one direction or another too quickly, will only exacerbate the trouble. After all, that is how the problems probably began.

Making adjustments is not a one-time fix. It is something you must do regularly (which is what keeps chiropractors and mechanics in business).

In your life, you will constantly encounter situations that have the potential to knock you out of whack. Examples abound in your life and the lives of the people you know:

- Business "downsizing" means you are out of a job or, if you are the lucky one, have a job that now has half the benefits and double the workload.
- Your spouse says, "We need to talk." What follows hits you like a sledgehammer.
- The results are in on your medical exam. "Are you sitting down?"
- A family member has been diagnosed with a "condition."
- What you thought was a smart investment evaporates right before your very eyes.

Those are some serious real-life issues: any one of those scenarios packs a punch that would understandably knock any of us on our keister. But the impact of such a blow and the duration of devastation are lessened if our response is deliberate, yet spontaneous and purposeful. In other words, you are better equipped to handle any situation when you start with the proper forward posture and perspective. And, as the events are unfolding, the adjustments required to restore your well-being will be less extreme because you started with a strong foundation. Your lifestyle takes on a self-healing characteristic, and you develop the ability to shift your perception from the negative to the positive, finding value and meaning in even the most difficult situations.

Sometimes, adjustments aren't dictated by our environment so much as by our inner desire for growth. But when we decide we want to make a change in our lives, we often go overboard and try to change everything at once. Consider that with the beginning of each New Year we experience the thrill of a fresh start and the chance to remake or rekindle a wanting aspect of our life. When it comes to making these changes and maintaining them, most of us have a history of failed attempts. Well-intentioned resolutions are often difficult to sustain and are soon abandoned. Why is that?

With the New Year's mind-set, you resolve to take action. You decide that this year things will be different. And wanting to accomplish your transformation as soon as possible, you decide to make a number of immediate and radical adjustments, possibly in multiple areas of your life. Making so many adjustments at once is, of course, a recipe for failure. Your exuberance pulls you off balance but in a dramatic and undesirable way, as you neglect important aspects of your life while you focus on your resolutions.

The way to make lasting changes in your life is to start with one small adjustment. Make one change you can implement and sustain. Once this takes hold in your life, you will see the impact it has on your overall well-being. Now that you have some momentum, a forward life posture, you can go further, making other adjustments to continue your progress.

The Question of Purpose

The phrase *on purpose* conveys two simultaneous connotations: bringing a sense of meaning to your life and performing deliberate action aligned with that meaning. Decide where you want to go and what events and experiences you want to enjoy (those things that create meaning in your life). Then, having made those decisions, initiate changes in your life—see the opportunities (which will unquestionably appear) to make fulfillment and meaning possible and engage them through deliberate action.

When life becomes overwhelming, it is easy to focus on the surface disruptions and their immediate effects. There are aspects of life we just have to deal with, of course, but sometimes we mistake those necessary "to do" items as the essence of or the driving forces in life. They are not—or at least they shouldn't be. There is so much more to your life, now and forever, than the cumulative checkmarks on your lists. If you feel that your efforts each day are merely task execution, you will never experience true fulfillment. You must recognize and elevate the purpose or meaning that drives you to act in the first place. What is the point?

If we don't seek to discover this answer (and the answer continues to grow and evolve throughout our lifetime), then we are living a life that is movement without meaning. You need purpose in your life. Activity and action are not enough. To be fulfilled, your actions must be connected to an idea that is greater than your personal desires. Your decisions about how you spend your time every day should be congruent with your values and beliefs.

Life is full of surprises: new responsibilities at work, unforeseen health issues, changes in relationships, and unanticipated turmoil in many forms. Even when presented with requirements or circumstances that you didn't anticipate, you can make them purposeful by consciously deciding to be proactive rather than reactive in your response. (Boy, I didn't see that coming, but I'm going with it anyway.) To transform disruptive forces into empowering elements, you must make them your own. You may not be able to control life's details, but you can provide direction.

> When I was eleven years old, I learned to juggle at a renaissance festival. Soon after, my mentor (a 6-foot-4-inch performer named Mike Vondruska) became my performance partner, and then our duo became a trio when Lester McNeely joined the show. The finale of our act featured me atop Lester's shoulders, Lester himself being atop Mike's shoulders—all of us simultaneously juggling. It was always a crowd pleaser, even the day, on the King's Stage, when it all suddenly came crashing down. I'm not sure what started my unplanned dismount. All I knew was that I was descending rapidly from my lofty perch. And because my legs were tangled up with Lester, there was no way to avoid a full body crash onto the wooden stage. But for some reason, after I made contact, I sprung into a pose—albeit lying on my side with my hands outstretched—presenting the fall with a stylish ta-da! The crowd went wild. Without question, they knew this was an unplanned moment, a potentially disastrous end to the show. The audience responded, I believe, to the way we handled the moment, restoring a sense of purpose to the performance.

ALIGNMENT WITH PURPOSE

The question of purpose makes me think of driving. Imagine that you are driving your car, headed to an appointment and running just a few minutes late. As you maneuver your car through traffic on the highway, you enjoy the rush of energy—anticipation mixed with adrenaline. It feels good to drive this way. Fast, but not too fast. The car handles well, responding to your input, heading in the direction you desire. Then it happens.

Maybe your thoughts are occupied with your impending meeting, or your focus is trained on the distant road, preventing you from seeing what is right in front of you. Whatever the case, you cannot avoid hitting a monster pothole. The instant your front tire plunges into the pit of disrepair, you know you are in trouble. Suddenly, your attitude and your driving experience are both profoundly reshaped, and not for the better. It is immediately apparent that your car has been altered substantially by the experience. As you continue down the road, you can feel the car pulling—and hard—to the right, darting dangerously toward parked cars, curbs, and other obstacles. It is controllable, but only with constant attention and effort. The faster you go, the greater the effort required to correct the situation. You are unmistakably out of alignment. What was an enjoyable, even effortless drive has become a strained and stressful experience.

We've all been there. Maybe, like me, in such a circumstance you have intentionally tried to hit other potholes in the hope that you could somehow knock your car back into shape. If not, don't bother. Trust me, it only makes matters worse. No. The only thing that can restore your car to its old form and return you to a state of effortless handling is a trip to the mechanic. You are in need of a front-end alignment.

This analogy speaks to me about life. There are times when we move through life with ease and agility. Our thoughts steer our actions with precision and expert timing. We bank into turns, moving gracefully from one encounter to the next with the unencumbered ability to express our thoughts and feelings. Other people seem to respond to us with helpful attitudes and a sense of relief. They are willing to help us continue our journey forward, offering directions, assistance, and encouragement. Or, at the very least, they are happy to get out of our way.

But when we hit life's unexpected potholes, the unforeseen and unpleasant challenges, our "driving experience" can change in an instant. Simple decisions are suddenly complicated. Making forward progress, even a short distance down the road, requires three extra turns and another tank of gas. What was once effortless now requires constant exertion. We are uncertain, and other people know it. Our lack of confidence stimulates doubtful looks, second guesses, and uncooperative responses from the people we hope will help us. Why is this? We are obviously out of alignment with our purpose. Fortunately, we can remedy this and adjust our orientation by refocusing on our priorities or clarifying our intentions.

Off Balance On Purpose and the Alternatives

When I propose that you live off balance on purpose, I am talking about what I call your *life posture*. You need to *lean forward* with your thinking, your actions, and your recognition of important moments, as well as with the way you exert your influence in order to generate a personal momentum that can come only from deliberate action. You should be off balance. Read the lists that follow and answer the question, "Which do I want?"

BALANCE VS. OFF BALANCE

Balance	Off Balance
Stagnation	Growth and action
Sameness	Change
Protecting what is	Embracing what might be
Imaginary/unrealistic	Real/our natural state of being
Having a little of everything	Having more of what truly matters

Being unquestionably off balance is more than okay—it's the way it's supposed to be. And should you learn to make the most of it, you can find a new capacity to manage missteps and create your desired future. You'll have greater energy, building momentum for your life that will propel you to greater (outward) successes and heightened (inward) fulfillment. And along the journey, you'll inspire others with your actions.

Or not. What's the alternative to being off balance on purpose? If we don't strike this posture with our thoughts and actions, then what "default" relationship do we have with our world and the people in it? The following alternatives may be familiar to you:

Off Balance Off Purpose—You are off balance, all right, but there is nothing fulfilling or directed about it. You attempt to respond to the chaotic events around you. The trouble is, you are always one step behind. Life seems out of control, and your actions bring no sense of meaning, joy, or accomplishment. To fill the void, some people in this condition seek pleasure through escapism and, in advanced cases, become addicted to unhealthy activities or substances.

On Balance Off Purpose—You are diligently working to maintain and protect a false balance. The only way to feel like you are winning this proposition is to constrict your life experience to an increasingly narrow view. (In order for my world to make sense, I have to shut out all but a few ideas, responsibilities, relationships, and activities.) Genuine opportunities often go unconsidered or are cast aside because you don't feel you have the resources to deal with them. They represent disrupters to your fragile state of security. In the process of maintaining this false front, you lose sight of who you are, why you do what you do, and any connection to a compelling mission. Life becomes routine, boring, and unsatisfying.

On Balance On Purpose—You are connected to your values and mission, but again, you remain so narrowly constrained that you will never grow to experience true and complete satisfaction. The focus becomes: "I have a good thing going here. Better not rock the boat." You have created your version of the perfect life with safe boundaries and limited requirements for happiness. Every thing is in its place, and you fight to keep disruptions at bay. This situation and the previous one are created by the scarcity mind-set, that is, the belief that opportunities are limited so you need to protect what little you have before anyone tries to take it from you.

Off Balance By Accident—"Anywhere the wind blows, that's all right with me," says the free spirit who is quite comfortable when off balance. If this is you, you enjoy the fact that life is constantly unfolding into new experiences. That's great. But if your path is exclusively accidental, you are missing an opportunity to experience real satisfaction. This condition is a natural phase of life—consider the college student who can't decide on a major or decides to backpack across Europe to "find himself." It's fun for a while, but most people eventually graduate from this phase of life to find a direction to their paths. Seek to discover what you were meant to do then inject that purpose, or mission, into your life. Otherwise, life becomes a "joy ride," and you are repeatedly left thinking: "That was fun. Now what? Can't wait to find out." Sometimes, the freewheeler becomes a freeloader and imposes on others for life's necessities. When those around become enablers, it becomes even more difficult to discover self-direction.

Off Balance On Demand—You are living by someone else's values, goals, and beliefs. In the process of trying to be all things to all people, you lose sight of who you are. Satisfaction stems from external sources and the validation that what you did pleased someone else. You can easily see how this powerless condition subordinates your enjoyment of life as well as your sense of worth. The classic example of this situation is the woman who has spent years focusing on her spouse, children, and household and no longer knows who she is. When the nest empties and the next chapter of life begins, she is left wondering what to do. Similarly, the demands of your job can become a substitute for purpose, whether or not they have a direct relationship to your values, desires, and dreams. When you define who you are by what you do, true satisfaction takes a backseat to business.

Throughout this book, I will guide you through the process of reorganizing your thinking as well as your objectives. As you do, you'll gain a heightened understanding of the factors at work in your life and your ability to improve your orientation and effectiveness. I'm not trying to radically reshape your life here. We are just going to make adjustments. Even a small adjustment will bring you measurable, and immeasurable, rewards.

We want abundance, not scarcity. Life's joys and positive experiences are indeed limitless, and so is your personal potential. Instead of a life that is pointless, aimless, or protected, choose one that is pointed, aimed, and propelled toward a compelling target, one that excites you, drives you, and thrills you to become better every day. If you are unsure of your mission at this moment in life, do not worry. Purpose is revealed to us when we ask the right questions. I'll show you how. And the answers come in layers. The great news is that you don't have to have all of the answers to begin. To engage life more fully, you first need to embrace its contradictions.

2

YOU MUST LET GO TO GET A GRIP

I OFTEN WONDER what alternate turns my life would have taken had I not learned to juggle.

Thinking back, it is extraordinary how that one event—the encouragement and instruction of my mentor—has shaped my life so profoundly. To me, juggling has been much more than a passing interest or an amusing skill. Over time, it became my path to understanding performance, discipline, and how to excel when it matters most. Learning how to face "showtime" and greet uncertain moments with hope and confidence is the real skill. Now, so many years later, I travel the world to speak to audiences about building these life skills to increase their personal performance. Yet every performance I deliver conjures the same raw emotions (fear, wonder, and exhilaration, to name a few) of my early performances, and I am forced to remember the first and most important lesson of juggling—and of living off balance on purpose:

You must let go to get a grip.

In juggling, as in life, you must be willing to release control in order to make something special happen. Holding objects in your hands is safe, but boring. The instant you launch those objects into the air, however, you create interest, expectation, and opportunity. It takes a willingness to let go and surrender to the uncertainty. At that moment, your skill, input, attitude, and attention enable you to craft a performance that is unique and real.

As in tightrope walking, focus is key to success. Before you make a throw, you must first look up and identify a target. Next, you learn to launch the objects toward the targets with consistency and confidence. The temptation is to look down at your hands—to confirm that you've made the catches—and concentrate on the results. Ironically, that approach—like looking down when on the wire—more often leads to failure and frustration.

The Illusion of Control

Juggling isn't about catching. It's about making excellent throws. If your throws are on target, the catches are likely to follow. But even then, it is not a certainty. Countless times (in both practice and performance), I've watched perfect throws bounce out of my hands, forcing me to scramble, compose myself, and try again.

When I began performing with Mike, he would introduce me to the crowd, and I would then deliver a short routine to demonstrate what I had learned. I wasn't very good yet, and my ability to "work the crowd" was even rawer than my juggling talent. But the "cute kid" element played well. These early shows, while only a few minutes long, became extended courses in self-improvement. The thrill and terror of performing challenged my skills, my nerves, and my willingness to surrender to the moment. Fortunately, I was oblivious to all of this, as we usually are during formative life moments. I was just enjoying the ride, trying to please my coach and avoid embarrassment. I found the audience was receptive, forgiving, and always encouraging. And one of the most profound lessons I learned from my mentor and those early trials was that every time you do a show, you actually do three shows—the one you plan, the one you perform, and the one you feel you should have done (the one you think about later).

We all like to feel that we are in control. In an uncertain world, we grasp for any sense of surety about what will happen. But the truth of the matter is, control is really an illusion. No matter how much you prepare, practice, plan, or ponder, you cannot completely control the outcome. You can, however, greatly influence the process. Your ability to execute capably and handle the unexpected moments with resilience and resourcefulness depends more on your thinking than on your talent. Some call it staying cool under pressure. I think it's more about the ability to interpret what is happening around you and to deliberately act to create a positive outcome in line with your purpose.

Getting a G.R.I.P.—Grasp Reality, Influence the Process

Guiding events toward a desired outcome is about making continuous, subtle adjustments. Over time, practice and attention lead to anticipation of what might be, and your actions become not only more spontaneous but also more on target. This is one of the critical benefits of living off balance on purpose.

To recognize which adjustments are necessary at any given moment, we must have the right perspective. While this fact is easily demonstrated with tightrope walking or juggling, it is often less apparent in our lives. We become overwhelmed by life's minutia, the endless events and tenacious "to dos" that have become our reality. At these moments it becomes difficult, if not impossible, to feel at peace and certain that our actions truly matter. No wonder—we are looking at our hands.

"Keep looking up" is a mantra that reminds us to rise above the outward distractions and imposed definitions of what is important and decide for ourselves what really matters. We must stay fixed on the purpose that drives our actions, on what is more vital than our moment-to-moment experiences, our daily operations. This means establishing and regularly connecting to guiding principles and a compelling personal mission. I'll help you do that in subsequent chapters.

To achieve this state of spontaneous yet deliberate and purposeful response, we must first dismantle our belief that we can, or should, control every aspect of our existence. Instead, we must learn to relinquish control when that strategy best serves us and learn to thrive even in moments when we have no clue what will happen next. After all, that is where we live. If the reality is that we spend the majority of our lives off balance, wouldn't it be useful to learn to embrace this state?

We must let go of the illusion of control because life is not static, and no element of your life is ever truly completed. In fact, life is a lot like laundry. It is never "done" or perfectly configured. It is constantly in flow. You are wearing some clothes, shedding others. No matter how organized you are, you will always find towels, T-shirts, underwear, and trousers you need to sort out, and clean. Even when you think you have completed your laundry, it is a fleeting condition. You soon find other items you neglected. Then there are the clothes you were wearing *while* you did the laundry. Unless you are doing your wash in the buff, you'll always have some unfinished business. When the clothes come out of the dryer, you think you are done and can move on. But no, you have a mountain of folding before you. And there's still ironing to be done (your favorite shirt looks like a shar-pei puppy). And what happened to the matching socks? It's one of life's mysteries.

Life is like laundry because it is fluid and the outcome is uncertain. Even when you think you have completed certain tasks or addressed certain issues, you often realize there is much more to come. Even when you think you've done a perfect job of sorting, you end up with a red sock in a load of whites. So you must let go of the idea of ever being "done" with your life issues and let go of the idea of ever truly controlling the future.

In the process of letting go, you begin to get a G.R.I.P.—a never-ending two-step of first *grasping reality* and then *influencing the process*. "Grasping reality" is the equivalent of telling a friend (or telling yourself) to "Get a grip," the root of the acronym. We recognize a gap between our present mental state or our perception and what is actually happening. It's tough, but by expanding your view beyond your intimate and emotional connection with life, you begin to see the events around you as they are, without exaggeration, judgment, or self-deception. Grasping reality also means understanding your capabilities, your resources, and your opposition, that is, the obstacles that threaten your efforts. It means being honest with yourself.

With an accurate picture of the real-world situation, you can better understand how you can influence the process—taking deliberate action toward a positive outcome through subtle adjustments. Every situation is unique. At times, the proper adjustment will be as subtle (but nonetheless significant) as taking responsibility for the situation or circumstances. Maybe you will recognize a behavior that needs pruning or a step you can take toward personal growth. When other people are involved, perhaps you can offer useful assistance, expertise, words of encouragement, a supportive smile, an attentive ear, an accurate observation, a timely question, or an unexpected answer. There is almost always an action you can take to influence the process in a positive way.

Deliberately Disengaged

Take a minute to reflect on the way couples react when they get engaged to be married. What a joyous, thrilling, profoundly frightening moment that is. And what do they usually do after they announce their engagement? Celebrate, of course. When is the engagement party?

Engagements are to be celebrated, we learn. And as we move through our lives, we likewise learn that we are expected to be actively engaged in or with a dizzying assortment of activities, relationships, and interests. We engage projects. We engage clients. We engage responsibilities, conversations, relationships, partners, hobbies, beliefs, workout programs, and even pets. And with each new engagement, we encounter the promise of new possibilities, increased joy, improved health, greater satisfaction, or at least some sense of purpose. Being engaged is critical to getting a grip because it's essential to influencing the process. And by saying yes to a particular engagement, we move forward with conviction and the commitment to deliver our very best efforts.

And we truly intend to follow through on our promises. But along the way, our excess of engagements overwhelms us, we face the ugly fact that we are not up to the task, and we lose interest, stamina, and effectiveness. We become disengaged, and very likely off purpose.

Disengagement is a serious problem that manifests itself in schools, workplaces, and relationships everywhere. Teachers are increasingly challenged to keep their students' attention. After all, how can one person, standing in front of a classroom, compete with the collective imaginations of thirty young minds influenced by technology and mass media? Workers are often more eager to surf the net, exchange text messages, and forward funny emails and videos to their friends than they are to engage in their work. People have become disengaged from one another literally, and in the extreme. For example, in the 1990s, one out of every two marriages ended in divorce, leaving the once enthusiastically engaged couple wondering, "What happened?"

So, yes, disengagement seems to be a problem, but again, I believe it is a problem of perspective. Let me suggest a challenging thought: Disengagement is not a bad thing. Disengagement is merely a symptom of what is happening. When we persist in trying to combat disengagement we are, in effect, staring at our hands when trying to juggle, limited by our restricted perspective from the possibility of grasping the true problem or gaining a higher-level insight that will take us toward a desired outcome. If disengagement is the reality that we must grasp, the question is, how do we influence the process, and thus get a G.R.I.P.?

In our classroom example, for instance, what if the question was not "How can we avoid unwanted disengagement?" but rather "What is it we want students to learn, and how can we innovate the process to achieve that purpose using technology, direct interaction, current culture, and other methods?" This shift may inspire new approaches and new ideas and thus yield better results.

At work, perhaps the question isn't "What are the consequences for employees who are disengaged from their task list and engaged in personal matters?" If we elevate our focus and take in the larger view, we might ask such questions as "Why do employees feel the constant compulsion to connect with others through technology? Do our customers, prospects, and suppliers share that same characteristic? If so, is there a way to harness the power of social networking (via technology) to create a fun way to regularly connect with the people who impact my business?"

With regard to our relationships, instead of asking "Am I completely satisfied with my partner? Does this relationship match my expectations, or is there possibly someone better out there?" how about posing some higher-perspective questions like these: "How does this relationship evolve and grow in a positive way? What is my role in ensuring that it remains healthy and vital? How does my connection to my significant other ultimately determine the person I will become?"

Ultimately, disengagement and engagement are just two sides of the same coin, which is why I claim that disengagement is not only not bad, it is also necessary. I believe that disengagement is every bit as important, if not more so, than engagement in our efforts to achieve personal goals, to grow, and to move forward through life. I am speaking of deliberate disengagement—purposefully and positively completely shifting our energy and attention among situations, tasks, and circumstances. We must disengage (let go) from one thing in order to engage (grip) another. I am not advocating detachment, separating yourself from your responsibilities. To be most effective in any one moment or in any one type of engagement requires that you be off balance in a specific direction, totally engaged in what is happening. But to do that, you first must deliberately disengage from what you were doing a moment (or an hour, or a month, or a year) beforehand. Deliberate disengagement should be a conscious choice and a discipline that is learned and even celebrated. Disengaging your focus is a vital skill to cultivate if you are to live a life that is purposeful, self-directed, productive, and fulfilling.

Letting Go

When juggling, once you make a throw (once you take action and influence the process), the object (objective) is out of your hand and out of your direct control. You must let it go; you must become deliberately disengaged with that object or objective. You must shift your focus to the next task at hand (your next point of influence). Successful people (and expert jugglers) shift their focus and energy from one action to the next, disengaging from the objectives that are, for the time being, beyond their immediate grasp or control. However, many of us aren't very good at this. It is difficult for us to grasp the reality that we aren't in control, difficult to become deliberately disengaged. We hold on to and accept more engagements than we can handle and then feel overwhelmed.

If you are to move actively and purposefully through life, you must learn how to let go. You must use the G.R.I.P. process and deliberate disengagement to help you focus your energies when and where they are needed. It is a necessary part of the off balance on purpose action plan. On the facing page are some examples of items that you may need to let go of in your life.

Perhaps you have been at work, unable to focus and perform because you are thinking about your family. Something you said or did the night before lingers with you, or you feel guilty because you are not able to be there at this moment with the people you love. That very day, you may return home to your family and be with them—but part of you remains behind, contemplating work-related problems, stressing about unfinished business, and planning your approach for the next day's efforts. In each case, your failure to disengage from things not currently in your control is preventing you from fully enjoying the present moment and delivering your best contributions.

It is in the moments of deliberate disengagement that we find inspiration. In that sense, it could be said that you must let go to get a glimpse. It is in the disengaged moments, when we rise above the frenzy of our daily demands, that we glimpse new ideas, new possibilities, and newfound potential. You have experienced this when you quiet the mental noise of constant thought, either through meditation or simply a deliberate effort to disengage from the world and enjoy a little peace. When you surrender to the empty space between thoughts, a new perspective on your problems is revealed. New alternatives present themselves. A pathway becomes visible where confusion lay before.

And, as you will soon discover, you are limited more by your thinking than you are by the ticking clock.

GET A G.R.I.P.

- Let go of the necessity to control everything. Expect an outcome, but let go of the expectation that it will happen exactly as you have planned. It won't! That is as it should be. Understand that you are a participant in the unfolding events, but you are not the conductor of everything and everyone around you. Whatever happens, it will likely be different from what you envision. As we grow spiritually, we also learn to let go and trust God or a higher power, expecting divine guidance and releasing our need to control events and people. Let go of ideas that are no longer useful.

- Let go of projects that just don't matter. Perhaps some of the tasks you've been putting off really don't need to be done. They just don't serve a purpose anymore, and you are merely going through the motions because at one point you decided that you would do it. Let it go.

- Let go of behaviors that limit your potential and restrict your growth. Cultivate new, empowering behaviors to replace them.

- Let go of negative emotions, such as resentment, fear, frustration, jealousy, and anger. Negative emotions are at times unavoidable. But they can also become convenient crutches that serve a warped purpose when they are used to justify your limitations. Don't play this game. Let that stuff go.

- Let go of the need to do it yourself. Seek the council of mentors. Find people who embody the qualities you wish to attain. Ask for their help, or imitate them from afar. You don't have to ask someone's permission to use him or her as a role model. Test your ideas by sharing them with others, even those who disagree with you. Delegate tasks that you are not good at or don't enjoy. Perhaps you should also trust others to handle tasks you are good at in order to free yourself to do what you were truly meant to do.

- Let go of the things you cannot influence at this moment. When those objects fly out of your reach, they are doing their own thing. Let 'em go. They will descend back into your view at the proper moment, and you will handle them gracefully when the time comes.

I know you have heard it before, but The Serenity Prayer by Reinhold Niebuhr captures these points well:

God, grant me the serenity to accept the things I cannot change, the courage to change the things I can, and the wisdom to know the difference.

3

"NOT ENOUGH TIME" IS NOT THE PROBLEM

IN THE 1963 *Twilight Zone* episode "A Kind of Stopwatch," Patrick McNulty does not fit in. His irritating personality and know-it-all nature win him no friends and even get him fired from his job. Later that day in a neighborhood bar, he meets a stranger named Potts who offers him an unusual stopwatch. McNulty soon discovers that this watch has the magical ability to stop time. When the button is pressed, all action freezes, allowing him the luxury to move about unencumbered until he once again presses the button and life's events resume. What does McNulty do with such a remarkable, valuable treasure? He screws it up, of course. After failing to get his job back, he decides to rob a bank. In the process, he drops and breaks the watch, leaving time permanently paused and ensuring that he will be forever isolated from others.

When I was a boy, I often fantasized I had a watch like this. Maybe you did, too. Surely, if you or I had this gift we would use it wisely, unlike Mr. McNulty. We would use the power for good—to avert tragedies, correct injustice, or at the very least clean out our garages. We would reclaim control over our days and create extra time as needed for the important and often neglected items on our perpetual lists of things to do. After all, wouldn't each of us be more satisfied and successful if only we had a little more time?

We bemoan the fact that there simply isn't "enough time" in the day. If we just had one more day in the week, we would be able to catch up on what we need to do. We'd have the time for all of the other projects that just don't fit into our "regularly scheduled programming." What would you do with one more day? I am going to go out on a limb and suggest that you would most likely do the same things you did yesterday and will do today and tomorrow.

How we spend our time is a reflection of what we value and, ultimately, who we are. So why would a "bonus day" change your nature, revolutionize your priorities, or alter your decided path? It wouldn't. No, I think you and I would continue onward, as we are accustomed to doing, content to spend our extra time chipping away at the same "living sculptures" we have been creating all along. A little more progress will be our only reward.

We have a codependent relationship with our concept of time. We need to feel the constraints of the ticking clock to feel motivated to move. We wake up and head into work because it is "time" to do so. We stop when the clock says we should, or we resent the fact that we aren't finished and have to work past the anticipated hour. After all, that means we will have less time to spend with our families, or to exercise, or to watch television, read a book, or visit with our friends. We set aside time for our spiritual development, trying each week to get to our personal places of worship on time (even if it's just the back porch); when that seems undoable, we often just give up and move to the next item on our list.

So we conclude that if only we had more time, we could certainly make better sense out of life and be more complete, balanced, loving, and useful. Time is limited. There is never enough.

Nope. Wrong answer. This is really a form of self-delusion. This mind-set has become part of our mental programming, and it is reinforced by external influences thousands of times every day. Marketers tell us that we need faster computers, instant food, speed dating, quick workouts, and shortcuts to spiritual growth. Turn on the radio during your morning drive to work and you can get world news in ninety seconds, traffic and weather "on the tens," and a stream of experts sharing advice in fifteen-second sound bites about relationships, money management, child care, sex, and of course, life balance. Each person offers a beautifully crafted and concise solution to a complex problem.

Should you try to implement their teachings, however, you'd likely find them to be incomplete, unrealistic, or inadequate. No matter, though: There simply isn't enough time to implement their advice, right? And in step the marketers again to play on these feelings, and again we look for ways to free up more time. We purchase any product that seems "faster," we work at more demanding levels (that eventually adversely affect our health and well-being), and we indulge in entertainment escapes to get away from the "rat race" of life.

The attitudes and belief systems we have constructed about time are unhealthy and untrue. Furthermore, they have resulted in two possible problems: feeling inadequate because we aren't getting more and more accomplished every day, or feeling justified because we have a viable excuse for not getting to the things that matter most. The most damaging of these is the belief that it's not our fault that life is hollow and unsatisfying. We can't be blamed for failing to maintain our relationships; there's just not enough time. That position is unacceptable. Using time, or a lack thereof, to excuse your life situation is a cop-out, and I sincerely hope you and I will stop doing it, because "not enough time" is not the problem.

You Have All the Time There Is

Living off balance on purpose is about harnessing time as a force to propel you toward your greatest aspirations. And when it comes to time, there is a completely level playing field. You have exactly as much time as everyone else does: 86,400 seconds every single day. Heads of state, high achievers, parents of eleven children, and multimillionaires all have the exact same amount of time as you do. Everyone is busy. While we cannot know how many days we will live, we can be certain that each one of them will consist of 86,400 seconds, or 24 hours. What you do with it is up to you.

The way I see it, you have two options. You can proudly proclaim how busy you are, taking time to recite a list of commitments and complications to anyone who will listen. Or you can stay focused, maximizing the effective use of your time. You can interact with others politely and concisely, then disengage from the conversation to turn your attention and energy elsewhere, taking care of what needs to be done. Which option do you think is going to get you closer to your destination?

Productive, successful, fulfilled people invest their time; they don't waste it. And they probably don't spend much of it bemoaning the fact that their time is limited, fruitlessly wishing they could have a little more. They use time as the tool that it is. They see the opportunity present in each minute to make a decision, to make an adjustment, to deliberately act in a way that will allow them to move closer to their purpose.

Using time as a tool is our effort to increase productivity, forcing more capacity out of the available hours in the day. It involves expanding each moment to greater meaning and usefulness. It's not about squeezing hours. It's about seizing moments. And that takes a different approach, one that enables you to slow down and bend time to your advantage. Sound impossible? Well, it's not.

TIME IS FLEXIBLE AND FLUID

We traditionally understand time as a linear commodity, an unchanging and unbending standard against which we structure our lives, measure our days, and mark our progress. While this perception resonates with our experience and offers some benefits (allowing us to keep appointments, manage deadlines, and hold our spouses accountable for their tardiness), it is insufficient and ultimately unempowering. Plus, it is untrue!

Time is not fixed, but flexible. Time is fluid, malleable, and ever changing. Time is relative. In his book *About Time* (Simon & Schuster, 1996), Paul Davies explained it succinctly:

> Einstein's theory of relativity introduced into physics a notion of time that is intrinsically flexible. Although it did not quite restore the mystical ideas of time as essentially personal and subjective, it did tie the experience of time firmly to the indi-

vidual observer. No longer could one talk of the time—only my time and your time, depending on how we are moving. To use the catch phrase: Time is relative. (32–33)

It is hard to imagine how disruptive and radical this idea was when Albert Einstein introduced it to the world. For more than two hundred years, the scientific understanding of time had been governed by Sir Isaac Newton's theory of "Absolute, True, and Mathematical Time." According to Newton, time was a rigid commodity, universal, consistent, unchanging, and linear. Newton's breakthrough provided a tidy explanation of time, which had not only shaped physics and mathematics but also shaped the cultural understanding of time. The trouble was, it didn't hold up.

Around the turn of the twentieth century, as we started to learn more about our universe and began observing and measuring the movement of material bodies and light, Newton's time proved incapable of explaining these observations, and the theory spectacularly collapsed. Einstein's work filled the void of understanding and explained that time was not fixed, but fluid. Time "bends" when subjected to the forces of speed and gravity.

While we may not be able to exert massive gravitational pull or achieve incredible speeds in order to bend time to our will, what is still true is that time is relative in the way we experience it. The five minutes you spend filling your gas tank are quite different from the five minutes spent in a passionate embrace with the person you love. The experience of watching a two-hour presentation on the history of tax law would be far different for me from two hours spent watching a well-crafted movie. The passage of time is relative with respect to our passions.

When I play golf, the four hours spent playing a round passes quickly because I love the game and everything about it—the physical test, the course, the companionship. My wife, Sheilia, on the other hand, thoroughly enjoys "memory booking." She will spend hours cutting family photographs and arranging them with borders, backgrounds, captions, and keepsakes from our experiences. While I enjoy looking at the books once they are completed, the process of creating the books would bore me to tears and seem to take forever.

This phenomenon, the relative passing of time, surfaces not only in our hobbies and interests but also when we are involved in meaningful, satisfying, purposeful work. When you are off balance, invested in those subjects, projects, and undertakings that cause your hours to "fly by," you will know you are in alignment with your purpose. Pay attention to this in your life. What activities cause you to lose track of time? When we are engaged in meaningful work, the quality of life and the way we value time changes. That is why you should immerse yourself in work that matters.

Time is also relative in the connections we make with others. You may choose to have a simple, businesslike conversation with someone in your life, which will seem like an ordinary, linear experience. But if you deepen your connection with that person by venturing into unanticipated conversation topics, sharing a laugh or a fun moment together, or discussing something that you or they are truly passionate about, then you have just changed the experience of the time you shared with that person. Now it becomes an encounter filled with potential, time well spent, and time that probably "flew by." And you may reap benefits from those few profound minutes spent together that otherwise would have taken you much longer to achieve.

We also tend to predetermine the time it will take to learn a new skill or make a necessary change in our life direction. Here, too, you are perfectly capable of adjusting your relative perception of time and the relative benefits of how you spend your time. Too often we avoid making changes or learning new skills because we think they will be too time-consuming. But if you make a choice, infused with purpose, and commit wholeheartedly in an off balance on purpose way, you may find the transformation to be nearly instantaneous.

Even more complex or involved skills can confidently be acquired more quickly if you devote increased focus and commitment to them, supported by a compelling reason. For example, I once met a man who told me the story of his friend who came to America and enrolled in college despite being unable to speak English beyond a few useful phrases. The semester was to start in six months, and he didn't know how he could accomplish such a daunting undertaking as learning a new language so quickly. My acquaintance advised him to get an American girlfriend, and he would learn very fast. The relationship, he explained, plus the impending start of class, would turbocharge his learning process. A year later he talked with his friend again and asked how it was going.

"Fantastic. I'm still in school, and I'm getting married," he told him.

"What?" my friend exclaimed. "I didn't tell you to do that. Don't you want to learn any other languages?"

The point is, when we are sufficiently compelled to learn, for both a positive and a purposeful reason, traditional time frames for learning can be dramatically shortened.

One other aspect that enables you to "warp time" is the ability to infuse one task with multiple objectives. This technique, which I will cover in detail in part 2 of this book, allows you to multiply the value of your time by ensuring that the choices you make and the activities you engage in are of importance for multiple reasons.

If the Ball Is in Your Hand, Throw It

In the book *The Power of Full Engagement*, authors Jim Loehr and Tony Schwartz make the case that we are not managers of time but managers of energy. "Every one of our thoughts has an energy consequence, for better or for worse. The ultimate measure of our lives is not how much time we spend on the planet, but rather how much energy we invest in the time that we have." So you see, "not enough time" is not the problem. Energy is the problem—and the solution. And that notion is critical in how we turn time to our full advantage.

Energy is a commodity we can influence, alter, and manufacture to address the demands for our performance. You can learn to become aware of your energy level (and the energy levels of those around you) and adjust it to be appropriate for the situation at hand.

One aspect of effective energy management is the power you have to harness momentum. There is a natural "flow" to life events. When we recognize this, we can align our efforts with our environment instead of forcibly (and often unrealistically) imposing our interpretation of what should happen when. This is essentially what we are doing when we strive for unattainable balance. The first step is to recognize your role in a situation and cultivate a willingness to take deliberate action toward a positive outcome when you have the opportunity. In other words, if the ball is in your hand, throw it!

This is a phrase I often use when employing the juggling-as-life analogy. Substitute your own sports analogy (baseball, basketball, dodge ball, or even a game of "keep away" on the playground at recess) and the point becomes clear. Life is an interactive proposition. When the opportunity to contribute your ideas, actions, and talents is thrust your way ("Catch!"), you are not supposed to receive the opportunity, set it down, study it from all angles, take it to a committee, and construct countless creative reasons why you should forestall action. Do that, and you are thwarting the very flow of life, denying your inherent rhythms and your interaction with the people around you. Now, that's not playing nice. Come on. Throw the ball. Take action. Get in the game!

Likewise, holding on to the ball, refusing to throw it, is the surest path to feeling overwhelmed.

I'm not suggesting that you act without thinking. I'm saying that you need to be clear about your purpose, because opportunities will come at you quickly. In fact, when you are clear about your purpose, you may find that opportunities present themselves more promptly than you anticipated. To deny them is sending mixed signals to the people who are trying to help you and, on a metaphysical level, to the universe, God, or your own concept of higher consciousness. We must be willing to act upon the opportunities that we attract, welcoming them with open arms. Even if the timing seems inappropriate, it may be absolutely perfect. How do you know if you don't act? Don't hit the snooze button on serendipity.

Once you are aligned with a sense of purpose, taking some action sooner rather than later to demonstrate your commitment is almost always better. Fresh ideas will usually be more persuasive and appealing. Don't suppress them. Voice them! Your excitement, even unrefined excitement, is contagious. You have a responsibility to share that energy and inspiration with your world. And when you do, supportive voices and significant opportunities will present themselves to join your choir.

A desire to postpone action is often a signal that you don't really intend or want to do something. Sometimes, it is also a sign it shouldn't be pursued. Your instincts might be telling you that it just isn't a good idea or, perhaps, that it isn't the right idea for you. In that case, you should let it go. Release yourself from the obligation of incongruent goals and pointless pursuits. Doing so will free you to pursue the challenges directly aligned with your purpose. You are unique, and you have a specific mission to complete. Uncovering that mission is vital to your happiness, so you need to listen to the clues.

Effectively Investing Our Time and Energy

Let's say you wanted to save money, and you were able to open an investment account (an annuity or IRA) with a $1,000 contribution. Every year you contributed an additional $1,000 to the same account. Let's also assume you were able to earn 7 percent interest in this account. At the end of a ten-year period, you would have made $10,000 in contributions, but your account balance would be $16,751.

It's easy to demonstrate when we are talking about money that setting aside a certain portion creates a huge cumulative effect, a positive and desired result. It's impossible to deny the impact of consistent action and compounding interest.

Yet when we talk about saving time, our orientation suddenly changes. We find ourselves searching for shortcuts, skipping interim steps in the process, and denying ourselves opportunities to savor the moments, explore ideas, or enjoy meaningful conversations. Time saving has become synonymous with hurried action, and that is unfortunate. And it's rare that we think about saving time in a way that takes advantage of how that "saved" time is actually used, or using that "saved" time in a way that compounds the benefits. What if you used the same mental construct for saving time that you used for saving money? What would that look like?

In this context, saving time would be a deliberate and sustained effort to invest small amounts of time (and energy) toward a larger goal. You would first make a decision that you wanted to accomplish something meaningful. Next, you would determine what you needed to do in order to achieve it. Then, you would decide to invest time at a regular interval (every day or every week, for example) into your worthy endeavor. Yes, this might require "saving time" in other areas of your life. For example, if you decide you want to become an expert in a new subject area, you may decide to invest your time by doing thirty minutes of reading each night, five nights a week. You could save that needed time by watching less television. Or, perhaps you begin listening to books on tape during your drive time instead of music or talk radio. Now you are investing time—and it won't take long before you see meaningful results.

The difficulty with this analogy is that the compounding interest cannot be easily quantified or calibrated. That does not mean that it isn't real. When we consistently invest time and energy into an area of our lives, the compounding interest is the exponential benefit we receive from that focused, invested time. In any endeavor—improving our knowledge, our health, our relationships, our skills, or our spiritual development—the time and energy we invest take on an increasing "worth" or "value."

Small, consistent investments of focused effort pay huge dividends over time. So why don't we routinely develop and demonstrate this type of behavioral discipline? Why do our best intentions often evaporate or fall far short of our intentions? The reason why this plan is more easily envisioned than it is executed comes down to two imposing opponents, each of which is standing ringside to tag-team your demise. They are the collaborating enemies distraction and fatigue.

DISTRACTION

Distractions are born out of a desire to be "balanced." If we decide that many things are equally important and tell ourselves to strike a balance among them, then when one of our pursuits starts to develop traction, the others each shriek for attention, "What about me?" Staying focused and productive requires an off balance attitude and an attitude that all things are not equally important. Remind yourself: "Right now, at this moment in my life, this is most important. It is part of my purpose. So I am off balance in this direction, and I'm going to maintain my focus and sustain my efforts because this matters to me, and I've made a commitment." (In part

3 of this book you will learn more about the process of self-expansion and how to minimize distractions and maintain your focus.)

Nearly every aspect of our world seems determined to distract (or refocus) us. Our cell phone not only keeps us accessible at every moment but also tells us when we receive email messages, alerting us with a vibration or tone. Trouble is, the phone doesn't discriminate or "screen" these interruptions based on importance. The urgent business message, the spam solicitation, and the long lost high school friend "poking" us on Facebook all sound the same and, unchecked, distract our thinking and actions.

Just staying informed about your subject, or world events, is an overwhelming challenge. Websites and bloggers abound, as it is increasingly easy to create a platform to share ideas. That's great, but it also means that information and the channels to share it are correspondingly increasing exponentially. Technology continues to keep pace with "Moore's Law," a 1965 prediction by Intel cofounder Gordon Moore, which states that the processing power of a computer chip would double about every two years. Not only is information constantly increasing, so is our ability to access and share it using technology.

With the full force of the Information Age assaulting you from every angle, it is crucial that you manage your intake. This means making conscious choices about what you will read, watch, and listen to. With every exposure to an information channel, you should ask: "What is the purpose of this information? Is it produced and distributed to inform me, sell me, scare me, or manipulate my behavior?" Be discriminating. Actively seek the information you need to further your quest, and leave the rest of it alone. You would be better off spending time in silence, nurturing your own ideas, than you would be passively absorbing the onslaught of messages targeting your mind. It is a battle for your thinking, and that is a battle you cannot afford to lose. Take bold measures to protect yourself from negative influences as well as burdensome distractions. Select and measure your information intake wisely.

The Myth of Multitasking

On March 23, 2006, Jonathan Sander was commuting to work, following his normal routine. He parked his car at the transit station and boarded the train. When he was nearing his destination, he had a sudden horrifying realization: He had left his seven-month-old baby in the car. By the time Sander switched trains and made it back to the parking lot, she was gone! Fortunately, other commuters had noticed the girl strapped into her car seat. Firefighters had opened the car and transported the girl to a local hospital. Luckily, she was fine. She was soon released—to her mother—and dad was left wondering how he could have forgotten something so important.

We have all experienced something similar to what Jonathan Sander went through, although maybe not nearly as extreme. How could it happen? Well, clearly Sander was distracted, preoccupied, and likely consumed with other thoughts and tasks. He was so "engaged" that he failed to recognize what was right in front of him (or in this case, behind him). This incident illuminates the problem with our overloaded lives. If this could happen to him, then what important responsibilities are we capable of leaving behind?

As a culture we celebrate and encourage multitasking without restraint. We exercise while reading, write emails while talking on the phone, and drive while handling a wide assortment of other tasks—among them eating, dressing, daydreaming, and (the number one champion in the multitasking Olympics) operating our cell phones. In other words, we are distracted. We have become discontent and unsatisfied if there's only one thing to do. We need several in order to feel fully engaged and productive. But the unintended results of our increased efforts and commitment to multitasking have startled us: we are less productive and less fulfilled. Quality and safety have been diminished. The satisfaction of completing tasks has become elusive, and we have become addicted to activity.

In 2003, the Human Factors and Ergonomics Society concluded that "cell phone distraction causes 2,600 deaths and 330,000 injuries in the United States every year." Hands-free devices don't seem to be making a measurable difference regarding safety, however, even in states where laws have been passed to prohibit cell phone use unless it is a hands-free unit. Perhaps that is because, according to a 2008 article in *Science Daily*, the danger is not as much about the hands as it is about the mind. University of South Carolina psychology researcher Dr. Amit Almor found that speaking and planning to speak were far more taxing to the brain's resources (and therefore, distracting) than simply listening was.

In the workplace, performance and productivity suffer similar hits from the failed attempts to do more things at once. Hastily sent emails sent to the wrong recipients or with wrong information can be embarrassing and costly. We also break our momentum with regard to one task in order to begin another or to respond to a request for attention. We may think we are being more productive, but that isn't the case.

"Multitasking doesn't seem to be one of the great strengths of human cognition," says James C. Johnston, a research psychologist at NASA's Ames Research Center. "It's almost inevitable that each individual task will be slower and of lower quality" (*Wall Street Journal*, September 12, 2006, Jared Sandberg). Human beings are lousy multitaskers. It is almost impossible for us to actually do two things at once. What we are actually doing is alternating quickly from one process to another. Each time we do, we break our concentration, halt momentum, and introduce opportunities for mistakes. Often, we divide our focus and miss the important moments completely or at least give them less credence than we should.

When you attempt to execute two tasks at once, you essentially create a new "one thing." In other words, you are not doing two separate tasks— driving your car and also dialing your cell phone. You are doing one task— a new task you have just created—called driving your car *while* dialing your cell phone. See the difference? The new task is a synthesis of the other two. Because this is a new challenge, it requires a different level of focus and ability. Consequently, your previous experience doing either task is not sufficient because the attempt to perform the combination changes aspects of the individual processes. It takes practice. And it's a little scary how many people are on the roads right now *practicing!*

So multitasking doesn't offer you all of the benefits you hope for. You attempt to perform new tasks that are amalgamations of other tasks. You take it for granted that you already know how to do these things, but you may not be able to perform them effectively when distracted by other processes. Essentially, you think you're "saving" time, but you may actually be creating the opposite result. Mistakes cost us time and other resources. That's why you should carefully choose when and where to multitask. You have to ask yourself, is it important to get all of this stuff done right now or more important that I get it done right? Is multitasking actually bringing me more enjoyment and fulfillment in this moment? If you are multitasking, you are very likely off balance, but are you on purpose?

FATIGUE

Legendary football coach Vince Lombardi famously told his team, "Fatigue makes cowards of us all." And that is true. For years, and in many studies, it has been scientifically demonstrated that physical fatigue negatively impacts performance as well as our mental abilities, such as decision making. Furthermore, a Bangor University case study published in the *Journal of Applied Physiology* in January 2009 presented clear evidence that mental fatigue is detrimental to the physical abilities (performance) of human beings.

Clearly, we are least resourceful when we are tired, mentally or physically. But our efforts to get ahead, to satisfy all of our responsibilities, and to achieve balance demand that we sleep less, push harder, and become accustomed to fatigue. It's just a part of life. Right?

Not necessarily. The people I most admire are the ones who have designed a lifestyle that is sustainable and self-renewing. Sure they are off balance—focused on a compelling mission and connected to a driving purpose—but they also realize that peak performance is a matter of timing. To be at your best for the most critical moments, you must be purposeful about rest, preparation, and solitude beforehand.

Renewal and Timing Your Best Efforts

Success in any endeavor is not only a question of how you spend your time, but also how you hone your timing. Consider the examples of professional athletes who tune up their skills and schedule their workout regimens in such a way that they will be able to deliver their best efforts when it matters the most.

Elite golfers and tennis players attempt to "peak" for the Major Tournaments of their respective schedules. The same is true for runners, body builders, and individuals in any competitive sport. By counting down the weeks and days to the big contest, they are able to manage their training, set their goals and targets, and incorporate periods of rest and renewal, especially before the competition.

In team sports, the players manage a similar process, and the coach and trainers face the dual task of helping each player achieve their peak performance, while also attempting to foster a team unity and winning belief that will be solidified at the right moment and for the most challenging tests.

The same is true for "winning" in business, in creative pursuits, or excellence in any aspect of your life. When the stakes are highest, you can plan and prepare in a way that increases the likelihood that you will be ready, rested, and at your performance peak at the proper moment.

How about you? Do you select your own major championships, the moments when you know you must be at your absolute best? Do you plan and prepare for those events, choosing to be off balance, biased toward succeeding when it matters the most? Do you invest your time to support these efforts, or do you let distractions dictate how your time is spent? Do you take a "balanced" approach, greeting every day with the attitude that you'll give it your best shot, try as hard as you can, and push yourself to the limit . . . again? Staying power takes endurance, but it also requires rest, renewal, and the understanding that some events are more important than others.

We try technology to save time and effort. And in some cases that is successful. But ask yourself, has your increased use of technology ultimately given you more or less available time to spend at your discretion? Or, do you find each moment consumed because, thanks to technology, you are more accessible than you ever have been? Furthermore, the way we use technology has diminished the time we take to disengage from our world, rest, and renew our supply of personal energy. We all need to fill up our gas tanks regularly (or unleadedly).

Life is not a fifty-yard dash. It's a marathon. We all face steep climbs as well as downhill moments. There will be painful, exhausting challenges and long stretches where you aren't even sure you are making progress. At those points, you need rest, renewal, and inspiration so that you can rise again and continue. The key is to continue. Every day of your journey, contribute to your momentum; sustain some forward progress, even if, at the time, it doesn't seem to be significant. The cumulative effects of your efforts will become apparent over time.

You set your own pace. And the pace you set will dictate your life experience. To experience a life that is hectic, frazzled, and out of control, set your pace to the maximum speed. You may find the adrenaline rush exhilarating, exciting, perhaps even fulfilling for a time. But is it sustainable? If you wish, instead, to slow down your experience and savor the passing of time, that is possible. It's simple. Slow down. Instead of trying to be all things to all people and handle every must-do item as if your life depended on its successful completion, engage life on your terms and at a forward pace that drives you without driving over you. Slow down, or if you want to get truly brave, stop everything when you sense it is time to recharge. Capture stillness in the midst of chaos. When we muster sufficient courage to cease doing something, our awareness of everything increases. It's almost like . . . well . . . stopping time.

4

THE GIFT OF THE GRIND

WE HAVE IT backwards. We lament the labor of our lives, resent and resist the effort it takes to get up early, face our commutes, and continue the disciplined routines we follow. We perceive the "daily grind" as an unfortunate necessity—an aspect of life we reluctantly must endure so that we may one day reach a moment of ease and comfort. When our hardship finally pays off and that glorious future is realized, we imagine, we will finally celebrate our success, enjoy life, slow down, and be at greater peace. Dream on. That's not going to happen, and thinking that it will is not only unrealistic but also counterproductive. It's backwards. Instead, we should celebrate the struggles, even as they happen, for the meaningful gifts they are. Sure, that sounds sappy. The truth is sometimes sappy.

Here's the deal. If you live your life thinking that one day you will reach a moment when you have attained success or captured peace and contentment, you will be forever frustrated. The only way to experience peace and contentment in life is to be peaceful and content with the process of living. And that means welcoming the difficult moments with open arms.

In fact, we should eagerly anticipate life's challenges, like an Olympic track-and-field athlete poised and ready at the sound of the opening gun.

Consider Carl Lewis, a legendary athlete who won a total of ten Olympic medals (nine of them gold) spanning four separate Olympic contests (1984, 1988, 1992, and 1996) and twelve years. His domination of the 100 meter, 200 meter, and long jump events brought him international recognition of his accomplishments and titles including "Sportsman of the Century" by the International Olympic Committee and "Olympian of the Century" by *Sports Illustrated.*

Can you imagine Lewis approaching his job with the attitude most people start their days with? Picture Carl lining up with his fellow competitors, positioning his feet in the starting blocks, looking up at the open track, visualizing the impending explosion of energy and subsequent strides, and thinking to himself: "Well, here we go again—another day, another race to run. Same old. Same old." NO! At the start of every race or every jump, he is primed and ready to go. Adrenaline pumping. Heart thumping. Brain focused to the sharpest point of concentration, thinking: "Let me at it. I'm ready. This is the moment I live for!"

In his mind and body, he had already run that race a thousand times. To reach such a moment even once, athletes spend thousands of hours in training. That time and energy invested—with sweat, pain, and sacrifice— is a prelude to an Olympic trial. Yet, even if that ultimate opportunity never materialized, the training was just as valuable.

It is unlikely you or I will ever have the chance to compete in the Olympics. Yet we face similar trials and training opportunities every day. How do you respond to them? You see, just like world-class athletes, those are the moments we should live for—the chances to test ourselves and perform. We need to celebrate the struggle. It is the struggle that makes us who we are.

Celebrate the Struggle

Life is not easy. But it's not supposed to be. No matter who you are, where you come from, or what you choose to pursue, you will face difficulties that test your stamina, abilities, courage, and mental toughness. You cannot avoid being tested. What you can control, however, is your orientation to those challenges. You can approach challenges with trepidation or excitement. Resentment or resourcefulness. Self-pity or self-empowerment. It is a choice you make not once, but continually.

Being a dad is my greatest joy in life. Like parents everywhere, I love my children immeasurably. I cherish their touch, their voices, and their ideas. The time we spend together is incredibly special. It's also, at times, frustrating, challenging, and testing. That seems to be their job—to test Mom and Dad regularly. Sometimes I pass the test. Sometimes I fail miserably. Regardless, there is always another lesson, another "pop quiz" coming up momentarily. And I'm the only "Pop" in the house.

When trying to teach my kids or redirect their behavior, I am amazed how much repetition it takes. Eddie and Maggie, my children, are wonderful, smart, and loving. But they continue to explore limits, invent loopholes in the family rules, and provoke each other. They're kids. That's their job. My job is to be loving, yet direct, creatively consistent, and always up for the challenge. But that challenge is as much for my benefit as it is for theirs. The effort is the gift, teaching me new skills, stretching my patience and creativity, broadening my own understanding of life and love. Every day, every moment is perfect and purposeful, although the meaning can sometimes be a little fuzzy around the edges.

Those fuzzy edges are a part of every one of our experiences. Often we begin the day energized, focused, and determined to accomplish something important or at least make measurable progress. Typically, those efforts are met with unpredicted interruptions and urgent situations that demand our attention and energy. Just the same, it is all part of a perfect plan, generously offering you opportunities to hone your talents. In the "grind" you develop your skills, learn to manage your energy, and clarify your focus.

In competitive golf, players savor the moments when they find themselves "in the zone." At such times, a player experiences a rhythm and command of the game that offers a glimpse of perfection. Everything seems easy: The swing becomes fluid and effortless, the ball achieves the precise desired flight path and shape, decisions are made with confidence, and putts seem to willingly find the hole. Even amateur golfers experience moments like this, which is why the game is so enticing and special. Occasionally, all of us become brilliant. And when we are, it appears to be so easy.

But tournaments are not won because a player stayed "in the zone" from start to finish. Such moments can be fleeting, and a PGA tournament spans four days and seventy-two holes. It is a test that is bound to have high moments as well as struggles. Champions win because they handled the poor shots and bad breaks with a level head, and they were able to find an internal response to match and surpass their external circumstances. Players call this "grinding."

When you are grinding through a golf hole, it means you are intensely focused and investing considerable effort. You are not in the zone at all. The game is not flowing effortlessly; it is, in fact, demanding extra effort. Yet, somehow, you are able to meet the challenge. When an errant tee shot ends up in the woods, you find a way to punch it out into the fairway, hit an approach shot that finds the green, and sink a twenty-foot putt for par. The result on the scorecard says you played the hole perfectly. But you know it was a matter of grinding it out. And you would never have been able to pull it off unless you had first put in the time and effort to develop and hone foundational skills. That's why professional golfers do so much practice grinding every day, hitting hundreds of balls and meticulously working on every aspect of their game. When the real test comes in competition, they want a response that is confident, automatic, and well rehearsed. And that is the gift of the grind.

I'm betting that you are not a professional golfer. But every day you have the same opportunities to develop habits that lead to consistent, deliberate action and discipline that will help see you through the tough spots that occur each hour, each day, each year. When you encounter challenges, mistakes, and unfortunate breaks, are you baffled or emboldened? Is your response based on preparation, flowing forth with confidence? Or are you simply "winging it," hoping for the best? Have you done enough grinding beforehand? I certainly hope so, because once you are in the heat of a performance test, it is too late to rehearse.

And remember, what you perceive right now to be a "daily grind" is actually someone else's dream life. If you can keep that in mind during challenging times, it will give you a useful perspective and an in-the-moment appreciation of your situation. Adopt the view that the times that test you are the moments you live for.

SOME GIFTS OF THE GRIND

- The grind helps us develop consistent action and disciplined thinking that have a huge impact over time.
- The grind stretches our abilities and makes us stronger.
- The grind offers opportunities in the form of repeated "failures" that lead to breakthroughs, often at the point of exhaustion.
- The grind teaches us about ourselves and refines our sense of purpose.
- The grind creates pain, frustration, and discomfort that help us become willing to change.

Foundational Efforts

You will not become a "master" in anything unless you first master the fundamentals. Study any successful person, regardless of his or her chosen pursuit of excellence, and you will always find a commitment to perfecting the simple (but rarely easy) skills and habits that form a firm foundation for growth. The reason so many people settle for mediocrity is that they are unwilling to invest the time and effort to fortify their foundation. It takes patience, persistence, and an understanding that an inordinate amount of both time and effort goes into the front end of any pursuit. It is through this practice that we stretch our abilities and achieve breakthrough moments. And rarely can we anticipate when those payoffs will actually happen.

In this regard, you simply cannot overstate the value of daily practice. A small amount of time devoted to improvement, coupled with consistency, becomes the necessary fulcrum for you to achieve performance excellence. Establishing routines to review and strengthen specific aspects or abilities programs us for ongoing improvement. Unhurried rehearsals prepare us for the pressure-packed challenges. Focused effort in short intervals triggers our thinking and allows us to strengthen between rehearsal periods.

When we think of self-improvement, we often think of exercise. Nearly everyone desires some form of physical transformation—losing weight, building muscle, getting "toned," increasing strength or stamina. So why is the U.S. population increasingly overweight and out of shape? It certainly isn't for lack of investment. More than 40 million Americans invest in health club memberships. According to the Sporting Goods Manufacturing Association, wholesale fitness was a $4.7-billion industry in 2007. That represents "gear and equipment" sold for homes, clubs, hospitals, businesses, schools, and hotels. People have plenty of access and opportunity to exercise.

The reason why so many people don't follow through on their desires for physical improvement is they fail to establish foundational routines. Making a one-time purchase (That's it—I'm buying a StairMaster!) or some other grand gesture (It's time—I'm hiring a personal trainer!) requires a single decision. But actually taking inches off the waistline requires more than the swipe of a credit card. It takes a way of thinking that filters our decisions and directs our actions.

Instead of joining a gym, I think most people would be better off making the decision to park their car at the far end of the parking lot when they arrive at work. This one change would create a ripple effect that would trigger other positive changes. But the key to effectiveness would be repetition—a commitment to follow through every single day with this small, but purposeful action. Suddenly, your orientation to "parking" changes. Parking now becomes an opportunity to capture a few minutes of exercise. It is such a small change that it hardly seems worthwhile, yet the key to creating measurable results is consistent, daily repetition.

Running late? Doesn't matter. Park at the back of the lot and walk a little faster. Raining? Bring an umbrella. Over time, you will start to notice that the walk becomes easier, something you actually look forward to. You arrive at work with an extra boost of energy. And you get it again at the end of the day when you return to your car. Going out for lunch? Now you are up to four repetitions! Not only is this new routine free, it truthfully doesn't cost you any extra time. In fact, it may save you the time you used to spend searching for the closest space. And the real benefit is the inner knowledge that you are parking (and walking) on your terms—a simple act becomes a demonstration of purpose as you silently exhibit your commitment to making a change in your life. The act of walking takes on a new, more positive meaning, so you look for other opportunities to do it. Hey, you might even start taking the stairs instead of the elevator. With a fortified foundation firmly in place, you have a sturdy base from which to take further action.

The fitness example is a good one because the method for improving any aspect of your life is similar to building a muscle. How do you build a muscle? It's a simple, two-step process. You must first use the muscle beyond its current capacity. Then, give it some time to recover. Both steps are essential. In fact, it is a foolproof plan. Once the muscle is pushed beyond its current limits and given the opportunity to recover, it will regain its previous capacity and then some. It will be better, stronger, and more resilient than it was before the challenge. This phenomenon is called supercompensation. The muscle not only will compensate for the increased workload but also will supercompensate, going beyond the previous mark.

This approach works to increase your physical strength as well as your mental, emotional, and spiritual capabilities. In order to grow in any of these areas you must put forth a taxing, beyond-the-limit effort. You must be off balance in a direction you choose and must exert yourself fully—often to the point of failure. Then, once you have "broken down" your muscle (or your belief of what is possible), you need to experience a "recovery

Supercompensation

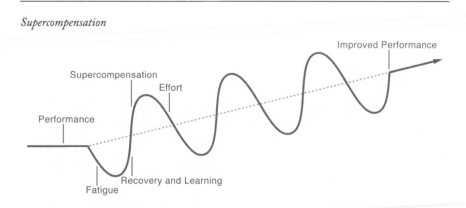

period" to rest, rebuild strength, and allow new patterns of thinking and action to take hold. In this way are breakthrough moments born.

Stretching Capacity

When people watch me perform complex feats of juggling and acrobatics, they often assume I have a "natural" ability. Surely it must have been a gift, something that came to me easily. It looks so easy for me to perform it now. Funny, but my recollection of those early days was not that it came easily at all. It was a grinding effort. When I first learned to juggle, I struggled with the simple challenge of managing two balls. Like many of the people I have since taught, I had ingrained a belief that juggling two balls was accomplished by throwing one up and passing the other from hand to hand, affecting a circular pattern of two balls in motion. While this was a successful strategy with two, it was inadequate when it came time to incorporate the third ball. I had to work hard to dismantle my old, obsolete pattern and adopt a new strategy of throwing and crossing both balls. Only then could I accommodate the third ball and become an honest-to-goodness juggler.

When all of my hard work paid off and I was at last able to manage three objects, quite naturally a new question consumed me. How about four? I quickly grabbed the fourth ball and attempted to perform the new challenge using the pattern I had just mastered for three. No surprise—I failed miserably. My mentor explained that in order to graduate from three balls to four I had to, once again, master a new pattern. The balls would have to traverse a new route to stay coordinated, circling back to my throwing hands instead of crossing my body.

Armed with this knowledge and new strategy, I returned to my practice chamber and once again attempted to juggle four balls ... with no success. I was back in my all-too-familiar "struggle mode." But then I began to notice something unexpected and truly significant. As I continued to practice with four balls, my three-ball juggling was getting much, much better. It seemed to be a side effect of pushing my limits. And the truth is I never really got the hang of four ... until I tried five.

If you think what you are doing now is difficult, it is probably time to try something harder. Once you do, the level you are currently at will become more manageable by comparison. That is how we learn. We never master one level completely, learn all there is to know, and then decide it is time to move on. Instead, we accept a new challenge and then find the resources—inside us and around us—to supercompensate for the new test. For example:

- Musicians practice scales at increasingly rapid tempos to grow more fluid in their playing abilities.

- Students take classes beyond their current level to facilitate breakthroughs of understanding.

- Parents have children (quite oblivious to the supreme effort that will be required of them) and then find a new capacity to love, provide, and function without sleep.

- Seekers of faith must accept a challenge or pursue a path without knowing the outcome. By trusting that the path will become clear, that God or the universe will provide, and then experiencing it firsthand, spiritual growth takes place.

- Lovers "become vulnerable" to one another, accepting the risk of rejection and disappointment, and discover their untapped emotional capacity.

A Catalyst for Change

Human beings are creatures of habit. With few exceptions, we resist changes that threaten our sense of comfort and introduce unpredictable elements into our lives. Particularly, we are unnerved by events we perceive to threaten our finances, relationships, status, and personal routines. This would not be a problem if our current choices and habits were delivering the results we wanted. If our lives were "balanced," there wouldn't be an issue with change. Everything would be just the way we wanted it, right? Too bad "balance" is an unachievable and unrealistic fantasy. Besides, it's boring.

Change is where life's rubber meets the road. It's where our innermost desires and long-envisioned dreams become realized. Buds of desire begin to blossom into tangible results. Yet, change resistance is so strong in us, the promise of those positive results is insufficient to inspire action. We are often more willing to continue behavior patterns that don't work than we are to venture into uncharted territory . . . until we have to.

Pain is the second-most powerful motivating factor on the market. When we face sustained hardship and experience pain for an extended period of time, we may become convinced we must change—that is, find a new solution to relieve our intolerable circumstances. For some individuals and certain afflictions, such as addiction, this becomes the only change catalyst that will work.

In a twelve-step recovery program, this is called "hitting bottom." When individuals progress through the stages of addiction, it is usually clear to everyone but them that there is a problem. Loved ones may try to induce changes. Employers may introduce counseling programs, issue reprimands for poor performance, or simply terminate the employee. The warning signs could not be more obvious, yet men and women with compulsive behavior view those signs as temporary conditions or circumstances that are happening *to* them, not *because of* their actions. Simply put, they are unwilling to change and will not become willing until they have hit a deeper "bottom," a condition that serves as a wake-up call and brings them to their knees. Sadly, this may mean losing connection to a spouse or children, facing catastrophic health issues, being arrested, or suffering financial calamity.

For most of us reading this book, the condition that eventually leads us to change is not so much willingness and courage as it is desperation. We all let ourselves fall into patterns of behavior that aren't aligned with our purpose, aren't moving us forward, or are destructive either to us or to those around us. Any behavior can become an unhealthy escape, helping us deny the reality of our lack of purpose and deliberate action, and our relationship to that behavior can become addictive and dependent. In such cases, the gift of the grind (the struggle and hardship of overcoming destructive behavior patterns) becomes tantamount to "tough love."

We should aspire to finding healthier ways to modify our lives and behaviors before they reach such painful proportions. You can become the choreographer of life events, instead of the hapless participant. But it takes a willingness to initiate changes and an enhanced orientation to the most powerful of all motivating factors. Pain may be persuasive, but it is no match for purpose.

Greasing the Wheels with Purpose

When you are oriented by a compelling sense of purpose, you will push through pain and hardship. You become unstoppable. For example, I bet you would be reluctant to run into a building that was on fire, filling with smoke, and becoming increasingly unstable. But what if I told you your most cherished loved one was inside? You would dash inside without any hesitation. What changed? In an instant, your purpose was defined, compelling, and greater than your sense of self-preservation. A compelling purpose, you see, is bigger than you are, and it can help you overcome almost any struggle.

There. After spending this entire chapter celebrating struggles and informing you that life is supposed to be difficult (and will remain so), I am finally delivering the silver lining, the good news, the light at the end of the tunnel: You can make the challenges easier. Just as our experience of time is relative, so is our experience of effort. What appears to one person to be backbreaking, tedious, pointless labor is to another a divine experience. A gift.

You are probably familiar with the story of the traveler who visited a city in Europe and came upon a construction site. He asked one of the workers what he was doing, and the man replied: "Cutting rock. It stinks, but it pays the bills." The traveler posed the same question to a second man who told him: "I'm polishing stone. I'm the best craftsman in town; just look at these beautiful edges." Still curious, the traveler quizzed a third workman. In response to the inquiry, this man smiled and stated proudly, "I, sir, am building a cathedral."

Isn't that a touching story? You've probably heard it before, but it does make a nice point: even a rotten job is tolerable when you employ self-delusion.

Sorry, did that sound cynical? Most motivators would have used that story to emphasize how our attitude impacts the way we view our jobs. I could have pointed out how our definition of purpose affects our experience and the quality we bring to our work. And that would all be relevant to this discussion. But instead, I want to ask a different question. "What do you think happened to the three workers?" Since this is likely a fabricated story anyway, I will now fabricate, to emulate Paul Harvey, "the rest of the story."

Ten years later the same man, let's call him Tony, was traveling in Europe. He was married now and vacationing with his wife and five-year-old son. His prior "cathedral experience," that one chance encounter, had forever changed his outlook on life as well as his career path. He was now a motivational speaker. He had written a book called *Building Your Own Cathedral* and stayed extremely busy offering seminars titled "From Stones to Sanctuaries—How to Love Your Job, Whatever It Is."

He wanted to return to the place that had impacted him so profoundly. So he ventured, along with his son and wife, a world-renowned scientist/supermodel (if you're going to fabricate, might as well go for it, right?), to the scene of the epiphany. The cathedral was finished now. It was lovely, although far simpler and more subdued than he had imagined it would be or described it to his audiences. As they walked around the church grounds, they came upon a man building a stone wall near a garden. Approaching him, Tony recognized immediately the man who had changed his life ten years before with six simple words.

When Tony introduced himself, the workman, Lorenzo, remembered their prior encounter and was delighted that Tony had returned to see the completed cathedral. "I'm surprised to see that you're still here, Lorenzo."

"Well, as I was building this cathedral, I fell in love with the place. I was taking such care with what I was doing, and I guess that was obvious to other people. They asked me to stay and maintain the church and property. So that is what I have been doing. I'm the groundskeeper. And I still love it. It is beautiful here, and quite peaceful. No more loud construction for Lorenzo! I'm proud of how it looks, and the people here respect me and my work. I'm very happy."

"Fantastic. Hey, can I ask you—what happened to the other men I met that day?"

"Well, there was Philip. He was a good worker, but he never really liked the job. So, he didn't last until the end. He decided to quit construction and start doing what he really loved to do, which was play music. Philip is a gifted violin player, but he never thought he could pay the bills by playing violin. Finally, though, he decided to give it a try. He was so talented, within a few months he was playing with an orchestra. And his passion was so strong, he also began to teach violin to children. He's become quite a respected musician, and he loves what he is doing."

"And the other man," Lorenzo continued, "Max, he was a master stonecutter. He always wanted to spend so much time cutting and polishing the rock that he worked very slowly. He was fired. But Max continued to cut stone. In fact, he began working with precious gems and diamonds, and he developed new techniques and tools for making perfect cuts without mistakes. He made a fortune and now owns his own diamond company. He imports raw diamonds and makes them into beautiful stones for jewelry. His work is highly prized by wealthy collectors and even royal families."

"Wow! That's great," Tony remarked, a bit surprised to learn that all three gentlemen he met that day were doing so well. "So everyone is happy. All of you are successful at what you are doing."

"Yes."

Tony thanked Lorenzo for his time and his inspiration, then snatched his son into his arms and strolled off with his wife toward town to continue their day of exploration. He couldn't help think that his observations a decade earlier had been incomplete. He was glad he had made the effort to learn more and gain additional insight. He then smiled, knowing he would soon be writing another book.

I'm not trying to be a Pollyanna with this story, proclaiming that every person's life will turn out rosy. But I do believe that each and every one of us can and should be fulfilled by our work as well as by all of the other aspects of our lives. We can bring great meaning and value to what we do and, if we follow the path of our true abilities, we can excel without limit, as you will see in the next chapter.

Sometimes, the solution to a workday funk is to change your attitude and view your job differently. Perhaps you've lost sight of the contribution and meaningful difference you are making in the performance of your job. Maybe you have temporarily lost sight of your passion. What was once full of purpose has turned into an obligation. By correcting your point of focus (by looking up and ahead rather than down), you may be able to make the adjustments to restore meaning to the madness. After all, each of us must go through rough patches, and the grinding is a part of the gift. Life is full of ups and downs—energy swings, emotional peaks and valleys, and setbacks of all shapes and sizes. That understanding might be sufficient to sustain you and restore your mojo.

But it may not. Sometimes, as exampled in the preceding story, your punishing grind is not a worthwhile regimen to be endured but a different kind of gift: a signal that you need to look elsewhere to find fulfillment. You need to find a path that fuels your passion, ignites your purpose, and gives you an opportunity to test yourself in a way that brings you closer to the person you were meant to be. Choosing the right profession (right for you) will accelerate your growth. And making smart choices about your relationships, your health, your spiritual endeavors, and your personal interests will do the same thing for you. You may continue to get up early, endure difficult challenges, and grind. But the grind is less grinding when it's greased with purpose.

When you associate a meaningful purpose with your daily pursuits (your work, your relationships, your health, your spiritual growth, and your personal interests), the path becomes more clearly defined and more enticing to travel. The gifts of the grind become even greater. In the third part of this book you will learn to uncover and cultivate purpose relative to all areas of your life. And as you undertake that journey and clarify what truly matters to you, the challenges will become easier and the rewards so much more satisfying.

5

YOU WON'T REACH YOUR FULL POTENTIAL— IT'S INFINITE

WHEN I WAS in elementary school I was not a great student. My energy level and enthusiasm were always ample, but they were not always aimed at learning. In the classroom, where I spent so many hours each day, I would routinely disengage from the teacher's curriculum and pursue one of my own—writing stories, inventing games, swapping notes with classmates, and simply drifting off into the world of my imagination. When it came time to participate in the class, I would do so. When tests were presented, I took them, and I generally did well. But when it came time to send home the report card to my parents, my teachers (bless them) would often include a well-meaning comment to accompany my marks. Something like: "Danny is bright but unfocused. He is doing well but not working at his full potential."

To this day, I confess, I haven't changed. I still have abundant energy. I still find it difficult and unnecessary to endure tedious and repetitive tasks, so I generally choose not to. Instead, I do the things that stimulate me and excite me. I create new games and explore ideas freely. And you know what? It works for me. I could not be successful as a speaker, author, and entrepreneur without those characteristics. But still, I am not working at my full potential. I never will. And neither will you. I'm not being cynical, but optimistic. Your true potential can never be "full" because it is infinite.

Yes, there are certainly limits to what we can accomplish. For example, I have so far been unsuccessful with my attempts to fly into the air like Superman. I can envision it, but I can't quite pull it off. At five feet seven inches, I will probably never become a star in the NBA (although Spud Webb did it with the Atlanta Hawks, and he was my size). Likewise, I'll never achieve greatness relying on my singing voice (just ask my wife). There are countless areas where my potential is limited or nonexistent due to lack of talent and, especially, lack of interest.

Talent deficits can be addressed and overcome with hard work and persistence provided there is a hunger and purpose to the pursuit of excellence. But apathy is a deal breaker. If you are indifferent when it comes to improving performance—you just don't see the point—then that is a neon sign that you are looking for your calling in the wrong neighborhood. Move on.

What we must focus on are the areas of our lives where potential is not limited but ever expanding. In these, our potential is infinite. In other words, when you tap into your true gift, your purpose, you plug into a source of energy and possibility that flows freely and forcefully, like a geyser that will never run dry. No matter how much time you put into a worthwhile endeavor, you continue to see new possibilities at every turn. This is your calling. This is what you are after. And even if you haven't found it yet, it is waiting, like an archeological treasure, for you to uncover it and claim it for your own.

We can either focus on life's limitations or explore the infinite possibilities. It's a choice—your choice. And what you decide, moment to moment, dictates your life experience and available options. It is impossible to act in a manner inconsistent with your thinking. So, if you are focusing on or obsessing about the limited and inadequate aspects of your life—the things you cannot achieve and view as limitations to your happiness—then you will act in a manner consistent with those thoughts. You will wallow in your struggles and identify with the disappointments. You will relish the idea of being a "victim" to external circumstances. You will continue to fall short of the life you deserve and are capable of living. Your thinking will be proved by your actions; it is a forgone conclusion.

However, if we focus on the aspects of our lives that are limitless, if those ideas dominate our thinking, then our actions will follow suit. Again, it is impossible to act in a manner inconsistent with your thinking. So, with an infinite mind-set as our cognitive operating system, we will see opportunities to expand our experience and our abilities. It's only natural. We validate and prove our thinking with our actions. It's our very nature to do so. So let's target some of the most compelling areas where your potential is truly infinite. That is not a platitude. I mean it. Your potential is infinite, ever expanding, inexhaustible! And it's yours already, if you will only recognize and claim it.

You Have an Infinite Capacity to Learn

Technology continues to deliver computers that outperform their predecessors with exponential improvements. It is truly remarkable how the machine I buy today is outdated in a matter of months because of a new processor, hard drive, or operating system. When it comes to storing data, you are no match for the latest PC or Mac. This is why these tools are so incredibly valuable. Yet, there is one area where you outperform your computer every time: learning new ideas. Mastering concepts is what allows us to turn facts into functions. Our thinking transforms data into decisions. Our cognitive capacity enables applications to become actions that bring about change in our world.

When it comes to learning, you will never run out of "disk space." You'll never crack open a book and encounter an error message announcing that your hard drive is full. At least it hasn't happened yet, and we've had some pretty extraordinary individuals push the envelope. Just think about Albert Einstein and Benjamin Franklin and the host of other scientists, inventors, and educators who have changed our world by learning more and more every day and then applying that knowledge in positive, unique ways.

It seems that a dedication to learning only increases our capacity to absorb information and ideas. Learning invites more learning and increases the speed at which we can absorb ideas. Cultivating a curiosity and appetite for knowledge seems to be a characteristic common among high achievers.

Thomas Jefferson was an avid, lifelong learner. His principle studies included law, architecture, history, and languages. He was an accomplished architect, inventor, legislator, and naturalist. He was a public servant: author of the Declaration of Independence, the governor of Virginia, minister to France, secretary of state, vice president, and the third president of the United States. At the age of seventy-six, he embarked upon one of his most meaningful legacies, founding the University of Virginia. He secured its location, designed all of its buildings, created the curriculum, and served as the university's first rector. How did he accomplish all this? Two factors: (1) He had a commitment to limitless learning, and (2) He didn't have TiVo.

Another modern-day example of limitless learning is a gentleman you probably haven't heard of, an eighty-year-old technology services technician named Bill Barnette. Bill was in one of my audiences, and meeting him gave me an inspiring example of lifelong learning.

Bill grew up during the Great Depression, attended a four-room high school with an outhouse, and joined the Navy in 1945. Because of his service and the GI Bill, he was able to enroll at Georgia Tech. When he first stepped on campus, he had never even seen a physics book or studied advanced mathematics, so his curriculum was quite overwhelming. But by applying himself and setting goals, he not only learned those subjects but also went on to graduate with honors and a degree in electrical engineering. This gave him the credentials to begin a career with General Electric.

When he was sixty, Bill retired from his thirty-six-year career with GE, where he had worked in the marketing department. He confessed that he had been grateful to end his career prior to the influx of personal computers so that he didn't have to endure that learning curve.

But retirement didn't sit well with Bill. He is not very good at standing still, and he quickly decided he needed some other challenges in his life. He tried teaching for a while. Then, in his late sixties, he decided it was time to learn about computers. He boldly walked into a neighborhood computer parts store and told the manager: "I'm going to work for you whether you pay me or not. I want to learn everything I can about computers." He did. And Bill found the learning enjoyable, interesting, and ever expanding. It was a fun challenge for him. Before long he was building computers himself. The more he learned, the more he wanted to learn about technology solutions.

When I met him, Bill had been working for eight years at a high school where students and teachers count on him for much more than maintaining computer workstations, networks, and equipment. They count on Bill to share his life experience.

Bill spoke to the entire school faculty at the start of the year and extended an open invitation for teachers to call on him if he could be a helpful addition in the classroom. He has talked with students about what it was really like to live through the Great Depression. When a history class discusses the Civil War, Bill can retell the stories he heard from his great-grandfather, who served in Robert E. Lee's army and fought in every battle Lee led. He shares his marketing experience from General Electric and even told the algebra class that he would take every test they did (without studying) to see if he could recall the answers. He wanted to prove that math is something you use throughout your life.

Bill Barnette is also active in his church community, claiming, "You are never too old to work in the youth department." One favorite lesson: He teaches young people the proper way to deliver a firm, confident handshake. "I've got a wicked handshake," Bill told me.

We've all been enrolled in lifelong learning, and the curriculum is constantly changing. As infants and children, we learn language, motor skills, problem solving, and the art of persuasion. In our elementary and middle school years, we learn writing, mathematics, science, sports, and history. We develop social skills that become more fully evolved in high school at the same time we learn advanced levels of our now familiar subjects. We also learn to deal with peer pressure and how to handle serious consequences of bad decisions. In college, we gain our first full grasp of independence and choose a major to study in depth.

During our work years, we learn skills and responsibilities in order to advance and earn money. We learn savings, retirement planning, and how to deal with health issues. We get married and learn that everything else we learned was wrong. Children teach us humility, patience, and the need for spiritual guidance. Old age teaches us to slow down and savor each moment. Declining health teaches us to depend on others and deepen our faith. Then we die, and enter an advanced program where we learn the greatest lessons of them all.

Although you accumulate knowledge throughout your entire life, you access and utilize the information that is most relevant at any given moment. When in your forties and contemplating a new career or experiencing a divorce, you may have difficulty accessing the information you learned to pass your freshman algebra class. But it's in there. You learned it. It just isn't relevant right now, as there are much more important items on the chalkboard.

Because you are a "learning machine," it is never too late to improve yourself or opt for a better, more fulfilling, and meaningful life. To say "I'm set in my ways" is a cop-out. That view mandates stagnation. In order to stay "in your ways" you must squelch your natural desire to learn. Don't do it. Open your eyes. Look around. And experience the wonder and curiosity that is your true nature. Learn something new today.

You Have an Infinite Capacity to Love

Just as we were built for learning, we are also installed with the natural programming to love. We are meant to love. Love is life. Love is truth. Love is faith. Love is our connection to spiritual growth. You cannot limit these things, so you will never run out of love. But if that is true, if love is available to us in limitless supply, how can we fall out of love? What limits our ability or our willingness to express love? Let me attempt to answer this question with a story.

In the center of a dense, African jungle a majestic waterfall roars. So thick is the surrounding vegetation that merely half a mile away its sound is diminished to nothing. Yet in its presence you can hear nothing else. Thousands of gallons of water spill over the three-hundred-foot-high cliff each second. The torrent is unbroken, constant, and simply awesome to witness.

Its volume is massive in every sense. Its beauty is absolutely breathtaking. And it never stops. At every moment, every day, the fall performs its symphony and ballet, delivering life to the crystal pool below. The pure, clear water is constantly replenished and could never be exhausted.

Surrounding the falls are three small settlements, each about five miles away. The first group of people had never ventured far enough from home to discover it. They relied on the food and water they could find within the confines of their camp, and on the rain that fell. This was adequate until a great drought swept over the land, and the people perished.

The second village had full knowledge of the falls and utilized the water to nourish its inhabitants. Over time, though, the people made fewer trips to the pool and relied, instead, on rainfall. Meanwhile, they constructed a huge wall to protect their settlement from outside influences. This barrier kept intruders and dangerous animals away, but it also served to separate them from resources. When the rains ceased and hard times came, they could not get to the waterfall because of the physical barriers they had created as well as their fears. So they met the same fate as the first group of villagers.

The third settlement viewed the falls as a vital part of their existence. They made trips to and from the falls daily, even when their reservoirs were in full supply. They maintained the path that brought them there with great care, ensuring that the relentless jungle growth would not restrict access to their water supply. The falls became a part of the village identity. Children were brought there from an early age to learn about this sacred place, and they were taught it was the most important aspect of their existence. As a result, this village flourished, even when the rains ceased. Their civilization thrived, grew, and prospered for many generations.

The falls, you see, represent the wellspring of infinite love, a divine gift. You cannot exhaust it. It is available to you 24/7. And it resides not even a mile away. In fact, it is within you already. To experience a life that is lacking in love, or to be consumed with love's polar-opposite emotions—fear, anger, revenge, jealousy, and hatred—we must build a barrier between who we are and what we were created to experience.

Perhaps, as with our first group of villagers, that separation is born of ignorance. Some people are unaware of the abundance of love that is available to them possibly because of a difficult childhood or extremely traumatic events in their lives. So, they plod along assuming that life is supposed to be difficult, confrontational, and angry.

But more often, as with our second village, we are well aware of love's liberating power and have experienced it firsthand. However, we create the separation by neglecting and ignoring opportunities to love. We construct walls to protect ourselves, building armors out of toughness, sarcastic humor, and skepticism. We become scarcity minded, defending the limited aspects of our personal villages—our possessions as well as our beliefs. And when the difficult times come, which they certainly will, we find ourselves ill equipped to handle them. On our own, we possess neither the strength nor the resources to surmount challenging circumstances, and we suffer.

Love flows through you, and it is a spiritual gift. While the subject of spirituality can be challenging for some, this is certainly not my intention. So let's simplify the spiritual question and define the evolution of your spiritual self as growing your capacity to express love all of the time, in any situation. As Mother Teresa once said, "Every time you smile at someone, it is an action of love, a gift to that person, a beautiful thing."

Mother Teresa also said, "We cannot all do great things, but we can all do small things with great love." She proved it daily by ministering to what she termed the "poorest of the poor." On the diseased streets of Calcutta, India, she and her Sisters of Mercy routinely picked up the poor, dying people of the street, gave them baths, food, and beds to lie upon. Their mission was to love them deeply until they died. Her life of service is inspiring. Yet, when she was asked how others should follow her example, she never suggested that they replicate her path.

Instead, she always instructed us to begin sharing love and mercy right where we were—our homes, our offices, and our communities. In modern society, she explained, the "wounds" are not as outwardly apparent, nor are they as easily addressed. Internal afflictions, such as loneliness, hopelessness, and addiction, are much more prevalent than terminal illness or starvation. In her words, "Being unwanted, unloved, uncared for, forgotten by everybody, I think that is a much greater hunger, a much greater poverty than the person who has nothing to eat." .

As with the third population in our parable, you must recognize that love is the essence, the most important aspect of your life. Even when your reservoirs are full and things are going along really well, you continue to make trips to the source every day. You carefully maintain the path that connects you, removing the encroaching vines, thorns, and obstacles. And when the difficult, testing moments arise, whether they are people, changes, or tragedies, you remain connected to the source and realize that your response need not come from you. It flows through you. And it is always a correct one when it comes from the pool of endless love.

You Have an Infinite Capacity to Create

Both my children, Eddie and Maggie, are incredible dreamers. They invent games, stories, languages, and even entire imaginary worlds. And, at the end of the day, when I tuck them into bed, their questions, ideas, and creative impulses continue, prompting fascinating conversations and smooth transitions into their respective rich and colorful dream worlds.

When we are children, this inclination to invent and create comes so naturally to us. We fully embrace the off balance posture of exploration. We are far more interested in what comes next than in the certainty of the present or past moments. We are content to make it all up as we go. It is our natural mode of operation.

As we mature, we gravitate toward the ideas we can hold with certainty. We become students of the past—fact keepers, evaluators, deciders, measurers, and experts in subject areas. Our comfort with not knowing and active creativity is replaced with a desire to prove ourselves, form definitive opinions, and engage life situations with reasonable, proven, and measured responses. Our questions are exchanged for answers. The quality and quantity of our answers define our position in the world and contribute to our feeling of self-worth.

We could all benefit from a child's perspective from time to time. A young mind might teach us how to be more comfortable in uncertain situations. With a childlike view, we might see possibilities we would otherwise miss. Challenges would transform into games. And we wouldn't be so desperate to grasp an answer, hold on to it, and defend it from contrary ideas. We would recognize that you never run out of creative ideas. The more we nurture our creative impulses, the more capacity we have to create. You will never reach your full creative potential.

"But wait," you may counter, "I'm not an inventor, artist, musician, writer, or performer . . . I am not a creative person." While it is true that all of us create differently, it is absolutely false that some people lack this talent. We are all creative in our own ways, and we prove it daily by creating, among other things, thoughts, solutions, opinions, humor, relationships, opportunities, and our very realities. You are creating all of the time, whether you realize it or not.

In my first book, *Success in Action*, I devoted an entire chapter to creativity and explored the gremlins that infect our thoughts and diminish our resourcefulness and inspiration along with the catalysts that seem to accelerate our creative potential. What was striking about the list of gremlins was that they were all negative thoughts that we actively construct to limit our potential:

- A belief that we are just not creative
- A fear of criticism
- A fear of rejection
- A belief that we are too old or have other limitations
- A notion that mistakes are unforgivable and embarrassing

In contrast, the catalysts to nurture our creative potential are all positive concepts, focused on opportunities and exploration:

- Seeking insights from other people
- Finding multiple "right answers"
- Exploring "illogical" concepts
- Breaking "rules"
- Thinking like a child
- Asking questions

- Using analogies and metaphors
- Drawing inspiration from nature
- Creating an environment that fosters creativity
- Engaging in physical activity
- Practicing improvisation

Notice that the first list is not just negative, it is also full of ideas based on scarcity thinking, that is, the belief that there just aren't that many good ideas to begin with. To hold these ideas, you must believe that creativity is limited to a select few people, a couple right answers, or only ideal circumstances. This type of thinking fosters the notion that creativity leads to judgment, ridicule, and embarrassment. Our fears become engaged, and our self-protective instincts kick in, telling us: "Better not try that. It won't work and will only lead to painful, unpleasant consequences."

To activate your creative programming and increase your potential in this area, you need to shift your thinking to strategies like the ones in the second list. Embrace a different set of beliefs, one that says: "Ideas are everywhere I look! Inspiration surrounds me at each moment. There is not one right answer but many. In fact, the creative combinations and choices are unlimited!"

With that type of thinking (managing your inner process), your actions (outer process) will naturally transform. You will begin to seek and discover creative stimulus in the examples of people you meet and in the world around you—in natural and modern wonders. Ideas you wouldn't normally consider because they are outside the norm, are abstract, or seem unrelated suddenly seem relevant. You see similarities instead of differences, possibilities instead of problems. And ideas that don't work are no longer viewed as unforgivable failures. You don't dwell on them at all because you realize that another idea is right around the corner. There are many "right answers," and the "just right answer" rarely comes on the first try. It may be the third, the fifth, or the twenty-seventh choice that leads to a breakthrough moment. It's all part of the process, part of the grind.

THE INFINITE POTENTIAL OF MASHUPS

A current approach to creativity is the concept of "mashups." A mashup is the forceful combination of two ideas that don't initially seem to belong together. Mashups have existed throughout time; they've been critical in the world of scientific discovery, invention, and exploration. But the term *mashup* really got its start in music, taking two songs of different eras, genres, or subjects and mashing them together to create something completely different. Mashup applications have expanded rapidly in recent years to include video, websites, and even business concepts.

The thought is that two successful ideas, when combined, would create something interesting and exciting. The new combination has elements of both ingredients, plus new characteristics derived from the combination. And the key to the idea is the fact that it isn't a gentle attempt to take a little bit of one idea and a little bit of another idea (each watered down) and see how they work together. No. This is a full-on collision of two uncompromised concepts, exploding together with the combustible question "I wonder what will happen if I do this?" Sometimes it doesn't work at all. Sometimes it is absolutely brilliant. But the potential for new creative mashups is clearly infinite.

So the term may be new and trendy, but the idea has been around for centuries, and it has led to countless creative innovations. Here are a few of the many areas in which examples of mashups can be found:

Inventions—In 1780, Ben Franklin combined two different glass lenses to create bifocals. In 1837, John Deere combined leftover metal and a horse and invented the steel plow. Thomas Edison combined filament and electricity to create the electric lightbulb. The telephone plus a tape recorder became the first answering machine. The list, of course, is endless.

Technology—Examples include Google maps, open source software, the "all in one" printers (the machines print, scan, and fax), and my current favorite, the iPhone.

Food—Every new recipe is merely a new mashup of familiar ingredients and preparation techniques. Trendy restaurants specialize in bold combinations. Some mashups transcend the trend and become part of our cultural identity, such as Reese's Peanut Butter Cups, Tex/Mex cuisine, PB&J sandwiches, and burgers and fries.

Business—In Cincinnati, I came upon a business that was a combination bar and Laundromat called "Sudsy Malones." Bookstores have coffee shops, health clubs have juice bars, and many big box stores have children's playrooms.

When I decided to mashup my love of performing with my interest in motivation and personal improvement, I created a new, exciting career path and discovered my true passion and purpose. By pursuing both aspects, full force, I've developed a unique offering to the world. It grows and transforms as I do, continuing to inspire and challenge me every time I take the stage.

When I speak to young audiences—middle schools and high schools—I tell them not to pick just one career path. Pick two or more! Don't limit your potential. Explore all areas of interest, then look for ways that your pursuits might combine to create a new and exciting approach that is authentic, inspiring, and original.

You Have an Infinite Capacity to Achieve

Don't you just love to experience a sense of completion? At the end of a busy day, we don't mind being tired as long as we have the satisfaction of being able to say, "I accomplished something important." We want our efforts to be worthwhile. We expect struggles, setbacks, and challenges, but at some point we want to be able to say: "I'm done. The project is completed. I'm finally finished!"

Yet, as long as you live, you are never truly "finished." At the end of every race is another starting line. No matter how high you climb, there will always be another potential summit. Every delicious answer reveals a platter of new questions. So the question we eventually must answer is "When am I done?" In other words, "How much is enough?"

Achievement is a wonderful thing. Throughout our lives we set goals for ourselves and accept projects from others. These undertakings can be small (such as reading a book or cleaning your house) or daunting (like writing one or building one). The size of the accomplishment and the effort we expect we must summon to complete it contribute to our perception about whether the goal is exciting or discouraging, empowering or debilitating, fulfilling or frightening. And this aspect—your approach to your "to dos" when it comes to living an enjoyable, fulfilling life—is far more important than the specifics on the list.

I have long been an advocate of goals. Compelling goals can drive us to produce great results, envision and attain rich rewards, overcome challenges, and inspire others along the way. Look no further for inspiration than renowned adventurer and motivational speaker John Goddard, perhaps the greatest goal achiever of our era. At the age of fifteen, John wrote a list of 127 ambitious and exciting life goals. He decided at this early age to (among other things) explore the world, become the first person to travel the length of the Nile River from beginning to end, learn multiple languages, fly jet airplanes, explore tribal cultures, learn to play instruments, milk poisonous snakes, and read the greatest works in literature. It is worth your time to read his entire life list (available at www.johngoddard.info/life_list.htm) and learn about the subsequent accomplishments (John completed nearly all of his original list plus hundreds of other goals).

John once told me, "I think the problem is most people don't set their goals high enough." He believes it takes a bold goal (or many of them) to generate the internal joy and sense of adventure that makes life meaningful. In his eighties John remains an avid goal setter, achiever, and an encouraging inspiration to everyone he meets—a living testament to life's infinite potential.

They may not have compiled a numbered, detailed list, but most individuals have some sense of goals and aspirations in life. Delve deeply enough into the psyche of any person you meet and you will discover some deeply held ambition. Very few of us are wandering aimlessly, without any sense of what we desire or wish to do. Purpose is preprogrammed.

Where we falter, I believe, is in our relationships to our goals. Our orientation, again, is the biggest stumbling block. We see our goals as distant dreams, so far removed from our present reality that we will likely never attain them. Consequently, we become irritated by our goals, not empowered by them. We overstate the commitment it will take to pursue our purpose. The anticipated effort becomes completely intimidating. Even when we recognize our goals and decide to pursue them, we may form resentments toward the obligations we have that prevent us from realizing our goals now. We become impatient, discouraged, and victimized by our overburdened lives. Think about a goal you have set for yourself. When did you set that goal? What have you done to move toward that goal? Have you moved at all?

I believe we should shift our focus from instant attainment to consistent progress. When you recognize you will never exhaust your list of accomplishments, you can conclude that the process is more important than the goal. Sure, having goals gives us a desirable target and provides the motivation to move forward, but the moving, the process itself, is where we live. That is our life experience, not the goal. Isn't the point to make life more satisfying and complete? If so, then the answer is not in producing more grand ambitions. It must be in addressing the process that takes us toward our objectives.

What role do accomplishments play in your life? Are you defined by your accomplishments? Or are you energized and inspired by them? To uncover your purpose, engage life right where you are—by connecting more deeply with the people around you and fully embracing the plans and projects that you have put in place. The specifics of what you pursue are less important than the intentions behind your actions. And, as you engage life, the operative questions are "Where will this lead? What will I learn? How can I make the most of this experience?" not "When will I be done?"

The universe itself is infinite and ever expanding. As impossible to imagine as that is—infinite and ever expanding—it is true. What is even more incredible is that you are a part of it. You are infinite and ever expanding also. Every day, every moment, a part of you expands toward infinity. Do you manage this process or simply let it happen? Are you expanding your mind or expanding your bottom? Do you claim more of your infinite potential, or are you fighting nature and actively trying to constrict yourself—limiting your opportunities, constricting your world and your influence to a narrow view?

You'll never reach your full potential. But you can reach beyond your present limitations, and then some.

Part Two

YOUR LIFE PATTERN

6

FIVE SPHERES OF INFLUENCE

I HAVE TAUGHT many thousands of people to juggle. Often at my seminars, I also use juggling as an object lesson to teach the process of learning any new skill more quickly. We use weighted beanbags because they stop and stay when you drop them. I have conducted these programs for audiences numbering from twenty to two thousand. It is always a thrill seeing the excitement on someone's face when they push through the difficulty and make those first few successful throws. They feel the rhythm of throwing and catching and discover that it doesn't have to happen at a feverish pace. The tempo of the tosses is deliberate, but manageable. After all, there is space between the throws and catches.

The next breakthrough moment is when a participant begins to see the pattern. Looking up, they are able to shift their attention from the individual throws and catches (being a task-manager of the objects) to the wider view of the flowing arcs of the balls as they travel through the air (a strategic view and sense of purpose). They are amazed that when they make this shift in focus the throws and catches continue to happen. In fact, catches occur with greater ease and reliability. That seems counterintuitive, but it is absolutely true. When you stop trying so hard to make catches and simply look at the pattern, the catches begin to happen spontaneously.

The *pattern* is the term jugglers use to describe the relationship among all of the objects. It's the way everything fits together in the air. Especially as the number of objects or the complexity of the challenge increases, it becomes imperative for the juggler to define and shape a pattern of throws or actions that combines to create a cohesive and workable entity. The focus is no longer on the individual throws and catches but on the pattern, as if the practitioner is sculpting the air with purposeful movement. When novice jugglers grasp and hold this image in their minds and work to replicate it in the space above, individual throws take shape naturally, and the catches begin to happen with greater ease and consistency.

The pattern for juggling three balls is called a "cascade." Your hands make alternating underhanded scooping motions, throwing the balls across the body and upward toward targets above the opposite hands. As each ball reaches the peak, it loses lift, stalls, and forms a graceful arc before descending toward the catching hand. Each catch blends into the next throw, continuing the unbroken pattern—the shape of an infinity sign.

Getting the shape right is really important, which is why the first lesson is always to begin with only one ball—tossing it from hand to hand in this manner. By starting with only one, we reduce the pressure of the moment and allow each person to internalize and visualize his or her own

The Cascade Juggling Pattern

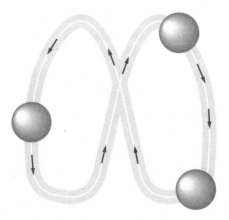

personal pattern. While the general shape is the same, each person's pattern will certainly be different. With a firm grasp of the pattern, you can then "let go" with greater confidence and incorporate more objects. By focusing on the pattern, you minimize collisions. The balls are all moving, but they are doing so in a manageable pattern that results in smooth, confident, purposeful throws and catches. The pattern is a healthy one.

As I learned in my early juggling lessons, when you progress from three balls to four, you have to learn a new pattern. The addition of one more objective (in this case, the incorporation of an additional ball) changes everything else and mandates a different approach and a higher level of commitment. That fact was even more pronounced when I graduated to the fifth ball. At this point, the pattern was similar to the first cascade or infinity pattern I had learned with three. The difference, however, was that each of the spheres had to be launched to a higher target. Instead of having one ball in the air at any moment, there were now three. These factors make juggling five balls feel more off balance than juggling three balls. When you're juggling three balls, only one ball is ever entirely out of your control, right? And it doesn't even have to be that far from your grasp. So with five balls, each throw had to be more precise, as there was less time for adjustments. You have to hit the mark on the first attempt or the entire pattern will collapse.

Sure, juggling five balls is much more difficult, but it is also more thrilling and fun. And the sense of accomplishment I experience when I do it well is so rewarding. I'm still doing it today, juggling five things. And so are you. You are an accomplished juggler of the five spheres of your life—your work, your relationships, your health, your spiritual growth, and your personal interests. And the movement of and connections among these five spheres create your life pattern.

Life Patterns

There are many patterns in place in your life right now. Some are intentional and others accidental. Some are useful and others debilitating. Some promote harmony and others foster conflict. We form patterns that guide the way we think, move, act, learn, speak, work, eat, drink, and sleep. Patterns determine the way we respond to outside influences. It is as if a certain situation, question, or proposition triggers an automated response. We've been there before, and we know how it plays out. So we follow our internal programming, our pattern of behavior. We continue onward in life, strengthening our existing patterns and managing life in a repetitious and predictable way.

But if what you desire is a life that is better than what you have right now—less stressful, less painful, more fulfilling, more fun, and more purposeful—then the patterns that brought you to this moment and your present life experience are insufficient. You need to learn a new pattern, one that will deliver better results. Otherwise, your life would already be exactly what you want it to be, right?

Your pattern is driven by your purpose. And even though the general shape of our life patterns is similar, each individual's pattern is different from all of the others, and that shape is dictated by the purpose we see for ourselves. To turn back to the juggling analogy, remember that jugglers don't look at their hands. They look up at their targets. Only by looking up and taking in the full magnitude of what is happening in your life can you begin to grasp the pattern and see your purpose.

When we are looking down at our hands (focusing primarily on the many surface-level activities on our "to do" lists), we naturally feel one step behind. We cannot anticipate what will happen next as we are looking down at what has just happened and responding to challenges as if they are isolated events. Only by looking up, or taking a more strategic view of our activities and life issues, can we gain more reaction time to exert our positive influence. And just as jugglers practice their craft to grasp the pattern, we can work toward an understanding of how the spheres of our lives can flow harmoniously with one another. With this improved perspective, it becomes easier to make empowering choices and take action. Because you have a clear sense of what your life pattern looks like and how different spheres affect one another, your "throws" are more consistently on target, and your "catches" happen with greater confidence.

Dismantling unhealthy patterns and restoring healthy ones is the key to life. And it is an ongoing challenge that requires thought, decision, and daily actions. But it becomes easier once we begin to glimpse what a purposeful life pattern looks like. When the patterns of our lives are healthy and sustainable and we have a vision of what those patterns should look and feel like, we can quickly recognize when the pattern may be disintegrating. We develop a sense that warns us when some spheres are beginning to travel outside the pattern, placing other aspects of life in jeopardy. With this early warning, you and I can make necessary, small adjustments instead of suffering monumental hardships. But first, we need to understand the five spheres that comprise and create our life pattern.

Five Spheres

It may seem like you have a thousand things going on and that compartmentalization could keep you sane. But in truth, you have only five areas of your life that require your attention. That's it. Everything that occupies your thoughts and actions is included within these fabulous five: your work, your relationships, your health, your spiritual growth, and your personal interests.

Those five spheres of influence are constantly within reach, each responding to your input and your efforts. Depending on the needs of the

Your Life Pattern

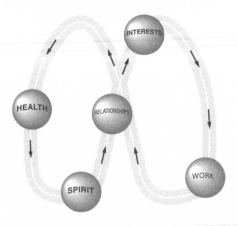

moment, you are able to control some aspects directly, while others remain "up in the air." Either way, the adjustments you make via your decisions, responses, and commitments determine whether your pattern flows freely or races out of control.

We are not seeking a balance among your five life spheres; rather, we are seeking movement of the spheres within a cohesive system or pattern—the pattern of your life. The ultimate objective, moment to moment, is to envision the spheres as one unified force. With a clear understanding of the pattern—what it looks like, how it responds and changes, and how everything is connected—you'll soon be able to make long-term decisions with greater certainty, and you'll even find yourself more capable of handling the unpredictable real-life dramas that come your way. But in order to begin that process, we first need to dismantle the pattern and examine each sphere on its own. As we do so, remember that the context for this discussion is you: your life, your current circumstances, and your dreams. Keep this in mind and apply your present situation to the text.

YOUR WORK SPHERE

When you meet someone new, and he meets you, it doesn't take long to get to "the question." Often, it is the first one that comes up: "What do you do?" It's a simple, harmless question, really. And it must have been anticipated. So why does it continually catch us off guard? Why do we hesitate before answering?

Perhaps we wonder if our answer is good enough. Does our "doing" constitute something that is impressive, meaningful, or worthy of a response? Maybe we are simply tired of answering it. Or possibly, the reason for our reluctance stems from another thought—a belief that, whatever the answer, it will be inadequate to properly represent the real "us"—the real "you." We resent that we will suddenly be categorized, sorted, and evaluated based on our answer.

What you "do" at this moment in your life is a choice that *reflects* who you are—an aspect of your personality. But it does not *define* who you are. The answer to the question changes throughout our life. When we are younger, the work sphere represents our educational pursuits—high school, college, and advanced education. We take entry-level jobs to help pay the bills. But clearly, this type of work does not serve as an accurate barometer of our identity. Imagine a conversation between two teenagers:

"What do you do?"

"I deliver pizzas."

"Fascinating. And how do you find that line of work?"

No, this evaluation process doesn't happen until we are older—after we have supposedly carefully chosen a career path and "made our mark" upon the world. By then, we should have "arrived," right? The question is, where?

As we examine our work spheres more closely, we see the reality of not only our present commitments but also our previous experience (like a rotating resume) and our hopes for the future. So many people feel that they are stuck in their present situation, and they fail to realize that crafting a life that delivers meaningful, exciting opportunities to work in a field they truly love is a possibility right at their fingertips. This isn't just an option; it is a mandate if you are to be truly alive and live *off balance on purpose*. Remember the story of the three stone workers from part 1? It's always possible to find happiness in what we do if we follow our calling.

According to The Conference Board, less than half of the Americans polled say they are satisfied with their job, a statistic that is down from 61 percent two decades ago. The figures are even lower among young workers. Thirty-nine percent of those under the age of twenty-five claim they are "happy" with their job. And job dissatisfaction leads, in many cases, to stress, unhappiness, and resentment.

Even the word *job* has taken on a negative connotation, as so many view "work" as an unpleasant but necessary part of life. I saw this evidenced recently on a bumper sticker that stated, "I had a life, but my job ate it." I know some people who refuse even to say the word and instead spell it as if it were some form of profanity. "That's my J. O. B." Yuck! With that mind-set, it's no wonder so many people dread going to work. They suffer intolerable commutes and live just for the weekends or their all-too-rare vacation days.

Instead of viewing work as a necessary obligation, I suggest a shift in thinking. As Abraham Maslow's pivotal theory on the hierarchy of needs suggests, the work you do serves multiple needs in your life, on a graduating scale of fulfillment. Once your most basic psychological need is satisfied and it no longer occupies your thinking, then you naturally begin to strive to attain the next, more advanced need.

The most basic need we fulfill is survival. We work in order to make money. That's a fact. Without money, we cannot eat, provide shelter for ourselves and our families, or obtain clothing. Once the survival need is fulfilled, we move on to the second level of Maslow's hierarchy: the need for safety. We must feel reasonably comfortable and protected, and in our world, money helps with that need. The third need is belonging. We work in order to feel connected to others, satisfying social needs for acceptance, love, and communication. As human beings, we have a longing for validation of what we think and what we do.

As job-related achievements bring success, we move up to even higher levels of fulfillment. As our job takes on greater personal meaning and responsibility, we enjoy increased self-esteem. It is also the means by which we serve others. If we pursue work simply for our own satisfaction, we are diminishing the importance of our efforts. Service to others can be a powerful, compelling mission that brings significance to your work. The 2006 General Social Survey from the National Opinion Research Center at the University of Chicago polled twenty-seven thousand Americans to determine the most satisfying occupations.

According to Tom Smith, director of the General Social Survey, "The most satisfying jobs are mostly professions, especially those involving caring for, teaching, and protecting others and creative pursuits." The most satisfying jobs included clergy, firefighters, physical therapists, and special education teachers. In each of these occupations, at least 70 percent among those surveyed reported they were satisfied. Authors, artists, and psychologists were also among the top tier of most satisfying vocations. In contrast, the lowest satisfaction ratings were identified with such jobs as laborers, roofers, waiters, servers, food preparers, cashiers, bartenders, and apparel and furniture salespersons.

The highest level of Maslow's hierarchy of needs is self-actualization. Our ultimate quest in life is to truly understand who we are. To experience the highest level of fulfillment with your work is to know that you are following your true purpose. Are you doing the work that you were meant to do? Are you putting all of you in what you do? When you find your true calling and pursue it with complete commitment, you will find that your work is not work at all. It is an enjoyable, exciting, constantly unfolding adventure, one in which you grow along personal, professional, and spiritual lines. For all of us this is the ultimate quest in life: to be aligned with our purpose. Unfortunately, many never know or even comprehend that satisfaction because they are simply doing their J.O.B.

Men and women all across America are drowning in boring, mediocre work. They are chronically overstimulated by trivialities and lacking in genuine challenges. Burnout is one of the chief ingredients for a chaotic, dysfunctional, and disharmonious life.

Naturally, people in this situation seek convenient solutions to make the problems go away. When people feel bad enough and sad enough, their need to feel better becomes almost a craving, so they do whatever is necessary to get temporary relief. What constitutes a quick fix differs from person to person, of course, but it ends in the same result: immersion in unfulfilling work just to get by. This type of soulless immersion can develop into a more chronic underlying unhappiness with oneself and with the world in general.

One of the keys necessary to any possible happiness in work—and therefore to success as well—is the self-knowledge it takes to know that we have found the right work for us. Work can be challenging or numbing, exciting or dreary, rewarding or disappointing. It's your choice, and it just might be one of the most important choices you will ever make!

WORK SPHERE QUESTIONS

- What is your work?
- What needs are you satisfying through your work?
- Are you doing the work you were meant to do? If not, why not, and what would you be doing if you were?

YOUR RELATIONSHIP SPHERE

In 1624 John Donne wrote: "No man is an island, entire to himself. Each man is a piece of the continent, a part of the main." This quotation has withstood the centuries because it is timeless truth. Each man and each woman is a part of the larger body of humanity. Our orientation to others, often in the context of family, work, and community, becomes the test of our character and capacity. It is in relationships that we express and develop our personality.

The measure of your life is not what you do for yourself. Ultimately, it is the impact you have upon others. Were other lives enriched because of yours? Were burdens lifted? Did smiles, laughter, and love take root and blossom? To say "yes" to these questions is the revelation of a truly successful existence.

Relationships are so vital that it is nearly impossible to overstate their worth. Without them, the rest of life's busyness becomes pointless, self-indulgent distraction. It is simply impossible to uncover or pursue purpose when we are self-focused. That is because your purpose is not about you, which we'll discuss in more detail in part 3.

Your relationship sphere is ever expanding and constantly changing, like the universe itself. It envelops everyone who has a connection to your life and includes your family, friends, coworkers, customers, neighbors, and acquaintances. Traditionally, when we think of "work-life balance" or read the books advocating the pursuit of that flawed objective, we think of work as a force we must balance with family. We are taught we must protect the family relationships from our work—create separation between the two. Furthermore, the relationships that are essential to our work life should be kept at a distance when the time comes to interact and engage our family. Everything and every person in your life has a proper time and place.

This is unrealistic, of course. Aspects of your life, including your relationships, are constantly overlapping. This is why I think of the category "relationships" as one that encompasses all of our interactions, both personal and professional. But let us examine the different types of relationships so that we may understand their unique attributes.

Family

"Family" is the category of relationships where we make the most consistent and enduring impact. It's also the area where we encounter sustained, unpredictable opportunities for personal growth. Within this special context, we take on roles and responsibilities that cannot be discarded, such as son, daughter, father, mother, brother, and sister. Bishop Desmond Tutu, African spiritual leader and novelist, tells us: "You don't choose your family. They are God's gifts to you, as you are to them." I believe this is true. Families are where people who ordinarily wouldn't spend time together (because of their vastly different personalities), are forced to coexist. But that is what makes them so valuable—they challenge us.

We do, however, make a choice about the person who will become our life partner—our spouse. Because this relationship is elective, as well as intimate, it is unique. This single commitment, which we intend to last a lifetime, is an evolving and complex journey for most people. The gift of all of these relationships is in the way they provide you with challenges and opportunities: the chance to learn, to love, and to grow your patience and understanding. With our family, we transcend our prescribed roles and get down to the essence of who we are as people.

A number of years ago, I was headed home after a successful and exhausting week apart from my wife and young son, who was then two years old. When I landed at the Atlanta airport and claimed my bags, I nearly sprinted to the car in my eagerness to drive home and be reunited with my little boy. I called and my wife told me that Eddie was playing at his friend Ben's house.

So I drove to Ben's house, unannounced. I wanted to surprise my son. I pulled up in front of the house and snuck through the backyard to the swing set, where I figured they would be playing . . . and they were. I was only halfway there when Eddie saw me coming out of the corner of his eye. He spun, stared, and smiled broadly. Then he turned to Ben, and with all of the enthusiasm his two-year-old body contained, he said, "Ben, look, it's my friend, Daddy!"

What a moment. What a thrill. With those four words, "It's my friend, Daddy," the time we had spent apart melted away. We were instantly reconnected. My son had reached beyond my role as his father and connected to the essence of who I was. That's the power of family.

Friendships

Friendships are another category of relationships, and this special group also provides a vital function in our lives. Unlike your family, you choose your friends. In doing so, you shape your own identity. We become like the people we surround ourselves with and claim as friends. This is why it is so important to carefully assemble your collection of comrades. It is also why, as our life changes and we grow into new areas, certain friendships wither while others take root. And this is the reason we pray our children don't get mixed up with the "wrong crowd." Our friends will undoubtedly shape our language, beliefs, attitudes, actions, and reputation.

I think it is important to distinguish between friendships and acquaintances. I have many, many acquaintances, and I'm sure you do, too. But, especially as I get older, I notice that my list of real friendships is increasingly compact. Why is this? Well, friendships require a commitment—care and feeding. We cannot claim to be a real friend unless we are willing to back it up with actions. That takes time. Also, we can keep acquaintances at a distance, revealing only some aspects of our character to them. Friendships require you to be more vulnerable. We need to be able to ask for help as well as to provide it.

The lessons and gifts of friendship are many: trust, support, sacrifice, new experiences, different perspectives, companionship, and laughter. Life becomes more richly colored, textured, and shaded when we share it. And the men and women we consider to be "friends" play an essential role in defining our experiences as well as our identities.

One of the most difficult, life-changing lessons for me was when a valued friendship was jeopardized because of my judgment and misplaced priorities.

I was in a position to make a difference in the lives of two of my friends. One of them, a talented musician, was itching to record new music that he believed would help revitalize his career. The other, also quite skilled in music, shared my friendship with the first. We three amigos crafted a plan to propel this project forward. I would provide the financing. My first friend would provide the music. The other friend would produce and direct the recording and performances. We would all share in the profits, if there were any, somewhere down the road. It was a beautiful, altruistic idea. But as time and the project unfolded, it didn't quite work out that way.

Expenses doubled and then tripled, causing me to take a hard look at this as a business investment. The artist became defensive and adamant about creative control, positioning my other friend—truly one of my best friends in the world—as an obstacle to the successful completion of the project. I got scared and my motives changed. Instead of doing the "right thing," I felt justified in doing the "smart thing." I met with a lawyer, drew up a plan, and took actions that I thought were necessary to keep the momentum moving forward.

I ousted my dear friend, squeezing his stake in the project and ending his role. Of course, this had a devastating impact on our friendship. Betrayal will do that. But it also proved to be a poor business decision. Many months and many dollars later, we finally had a completed record in hand. But because of the experience, the final product represented something distasteful to me. The music was good, but it conjured emotions quite the opposite from my original intent. I lost interest and cut my losses.

The fact that I had nearly lost a friend, my best friend, caused me to wonder how the heck it had happened. And those answers made me smarter, more humble, and capable of moving forward with reconciliation. Today, our friendship is stronger than ever. I'm on good terms with my artist friend also. And I feel good to have played a role in helping his music come to fruition. I've abandoned all expectations of ever reclaiming my investment. In that sense, this was a very expensive lesson, financially and emotionally. But you get what you pay for. This was one of the most important lessons I have ever learned: The value of true friendship far exceeds the value of financial schemes.

Colleagues

The people we work with are also represented in our relationship sphere. Our coworkers may also be friends or family. But even in those cases, the context of a professional environment requires a different approach to interaction. Why? There is work to complete, a corporate image to uphold, and in some cases, a political power structure to consider. In other words, there are a lot more rules guiding professional conduct. Our business relationships also extend to our customers, clients, partners, suppliers, and independent contractors.

Because we spend so much time interacting with these people, we should strive to form quality relationships. The success of our business pursuits depends on a network of advocates, clients, and talented people we can rely upon. While the dynamics of every job are different, I would offer a guiding principle: make it your business to help others succeed, and your success is guaranteed.

The power of our connections with other individuals, also known as our "relational capital," is a precious commodity. With it we can learn through other people's experience, significantly reducing our learning curves. We magnify our impact through relationships, marshaling support and engaging the power of numbers. Sometimes we face setbacks and need to rely upon our relational support system. If you wait until you need a support system to start developing one, it is all but certain the road will be difficult. As Harvey Mackay writes in his book of the same title, you must "Dig your well before you are thirsty." The time to develop a network of relationships is now, and the sooner you fix your focus on helping others prosper, the more your success is assured.

RELATIONSHIP SPHERE QUESTIONS

- What are the most important personal and professional relationships in your life?
- How are you ensuring that those relationships remain strong and continue to grow?
- Are you asking for help and willing to provide it when asked?
- Do you have friends who may be jeopardizing your positive growth? If so, you may need to address the situation. Ultimately, you may determine that it is time to devote less attention to those friendships and seek support elsewhere.

YOUR HEALTH SPHERE

How's your health? And what does the state of your health mean to you?

"Getting healthy" is an aspiration for most of us. We know it is important, even vital. But how? It might mean losing a few pounds, curbing unhealthy habits, managing our stress levels better, exercising more frequently, or giving up the lifestyle we have come to adore. But those specific choices and paths toward pursuing health are merely "tactics," means to achieving something much more important: a quality life.

Being healthy is the equivalent of "upgrading" every second of your life. When you are truly healthy, each breath becomes more satisfying. Every step becomes easier. You begin the day with more energy and confidence and enjoy nights of rejuvenating, restorative rest. Longevity may be a pleasant side affect, but the real aim is living this day and every day in a body that is capable, mobile, and strong.

Healthy behavior is such a critical aspect, of course, because it predicates our physical and mental well-being and, ultimately, the fulfillment of everything else we pursue. If we are unhealthy, our work and relationships will suffer also. Without sufficient energy, we cannot remain confident or optimistic or follow a task through to completion.

The good news is that the power to create healthy patterns of living lies within you if you can shift your thinking. Instead of viewing your health as a separate aspect you are pursuing in life, or perhaps a recreational activity you must make extra time for, you must clearly understand the intersections of your health sphere with every other area of your life. The next chapter will help you do this.

You cannot change bodies with someone else. Your genetic makeup and life history have brought you to the state of health that you currently enjoy or suffer. Life's unexpected accidents, injuries, or diseases also play their role. But moving forward, you do have the ability, as well as the responsibility, to influence your health in four positive ways: what you put into your body, the amount of rest you give your body, how you move your body, and what you think.

First, you decide what you put into your body. We all know what we should and should not consume. We know we should drink more water, eat more fruits and vegetables, and moderate our intake of detrimental substances like sugars, saturated fats, caffeine, and alcohol. Other things we know we should avoid entirely, such as tobacco. But a healthy and empowering life pattern goes beyond the understanding of what is best for our bodies by putting knowledge into action.

By eating well and avoiding unhealthy substances, we increase our energy. But another factor that plays a huge role in your current state of health is rest (the second positive influence I mentioned earlier). In a *20/20* interview, Dr. David Dinges, chief of the Division of Sleep and

Chronobiology in the Psychiatry Department of the University of Pennsylvania, estimated that only 10 percent of Americans can consistently sleep fewer than eight hours per night without harming their health. This news is alarming to those of us who cannot remember the last time we enjoyed a full eight hours of rest. According to the National Sleep Foundation, Americans average 6.9 hours of sleep on weeknights and 7.5 hours on weekends. Nearly two-thirds of adults report some form of sleep problem, including insomnia, sleep apnea, restless legs syndrome, and movement disorders.

Every person is different, and some of us require more sleep than others. According to Dr. Dinges, some people physically require nine hours of sleep per night or more to function without impairment. Habitual "sleep debt" has short-term and long-term consequences to our health and ability to function, affecting our attention span, mood, endurance, and defense against and recovery from sickness.

So why do we endure and even embrace a "rest-less" life? Simply put, we feel it is the only way we can cope with the increasing pressures and responsibilities that confront us. Even if we are consciously aware of the adverse effects, we choose to under sleep and overwork ourselves in an effort to keep up with life's feverish pace.

It's ironic that most Americans consider themselves "on the move," but they fail to move their bodies enough to attain the physical benefits of exercise. This is the third critical factor in our overall health, but it is the most often neglected. Technology, entertainment choices, and the type of work we do conspire to keep us sedentary. In order to move our bodies, pick up our heart rates, and get exercise, we feel we need to visit a gym and perform a thirty-minute workout. If we can't find the time, it doesn't happen, and we go another day without it. It doesn't have to be that way. You can incorporate movement into your lifestyle. You can go through your daily routine with an approach that promotes exercise, stretching, and greater health. Instead of sequestering yourself until you find time for a workout routine, look for ways you can improve your health while you live your life. Remember the example in chapter 4 about parking at the back of your office parking lot and walking a bit further every day?

It all starts with your thinking, the fourth and final way to positively influence your health. So, to improve your health, you need to first improve the way you think about health. Instead of viewing changes as sacrifices, you truly need to see them as exciting opportunities to gain something much greater—as cheesy as this sounds. Only then will you adopt the proper orientation to effect a lasting change. And with this mind-set, the difficulties and struggles are greatly diminished.

Maintaining a proper mind-set and the cognitive ability to process what's happening in your world is also a function of health—mental health. Your mental health is every bit as important as your physical health, and the two are inextricably linked. Mental health issues range from the day-to-day moods we experience, our stress levels, anger management, depression, and confidence issues to far more serious challenges that require professional care. Maintaining an empowering state of mental health is essential because it undergirds our experience of reality. Proper maintenance is a function of disciplined thought, useful habits, self-monitoring, and correction. The mind is an astonishingly complex and magnificent processing system. Our mental capabilities, if we cultivate and strengthen them, can allow us to solve difficult problems, overcome immense adversity, create new possibilities, and transcend even the most limiting physical conditions.

Mental and physical health are linked in a number of ways. When you exercise, you release endorphins that improve your mood. When you take time to manage your mental stress, you lessen the negative physical effects of stress on your body. Conversely, those who suffer debilitating mental states on a regular basis, living with the reality of negative thoughts, depression, torment, anguish, and other harmful mental states, may find themselves experiencing physical manifestations of illness and disease.

Our food and beverage intake also impacts our mental health. Diet plays an important role: certain foods promote healthy cognitive function, whereas others do not. But when it comes to mental health, it is important also to manage our intake of ideas, information, and influences. Surround yourself with beneficial, healthy, exciting sources of stimuli. Read challenging and inspiring material. Limit exposure to negative people and disturbing images. Focus your mind on solutions and positive outcomes rather than problems and impending doom. When you do, you engage the most powerful instrument on earth, the human mind, to create a positive and magnificent reality.

HEALTH SPHERE QUESTIONS

- What are three things you can start doing to improve your physical and mental health?
- What is one thing you can stop doing?
- What has prevented you from making these changes in the past?

YOUR SPIRITUAL GROWTH SPHERE

Spiritual growth and fulfillment are part of a lifelong, personal journey. In this discussion of your life pattern, I am not advocating a particular religion, philosophy, faith, or belief system. I am suggesting that without recognition of your spiritual nature, you are missing the most important question of life: Why are you here? To live off balance on purpose, I believe it is essential to contemplate, investigate, and pursue your God-given purpose. As human beings, we can never obtain a perfect knowledge of God, but it is in the pursuit of that knowledge that we grow spiritually.

I believe we are all born with a spiritual hunger. If you fail to embark upon the journey of understanding your spiritual identity, you risk having only a superficial existence. You will likely seek external means to satiate this hunger and bring yourself joy and completeness. For some, this pursuit leads to obsessions, addictions, and endless frustrations. That's because the full richness of life and the most significant achievements any human can attain, such as overcoming fear or experiencing peace, love, and serenity, cannot be acquired by external means. These treasures are discovered by digging deep, beyond your immediate self-consciousness and toward the realization of a spiritual relationship with a higher power. Personally, I am a Christian, and I am on a lifelong quest to better understand and act in harmony with God and the teachings of Jesus Christ. To me, His Sermon on the Mount is a perfect blueprint for life. It is not my intention in this book to persuade you to adopt my view, although I do suggest you investigate for yourself. A spiritual journey begins with questions, not answers. Ask bold questions.

Many people consider themselves spiritual, yet resist becoming involved in a community of faith. They say, "I'm spiritual, just not religious." To me this is an honest and widely held position, and one I adopted in my life for quite some time. The problem with this view, as I see it, is that it leaves you wandering without guidelines or the security of bedrock beliefs and principles. Also, this position lacks the accountability and structure that comes from having a place of worship and a fellowship of people who share your journey. To me, these relationships are essential for spiritual growth.

I have personally experienced profound spiritual moments in the middle of the woods, in connections with people I have encountered, on the golf course, in a Native American sweat lodge, in churches, alone, and in the middle of enormous crowds. God is infinite, limitless, and everywhere. Regardless of what you call it, your quest to be in harmony with this higher power is a never-ending journey.

I once heard Dr. Wayne Dyer make the statement, "You are not a human being having a spiritual experience, but a spiritual being having a human experience." I believe this is true. Your spirit exists separate from your body and transcends the limits of your physical form. Regardless of your beliefs, I am certain that you have had spiritual experiences. You know what it feels like when your spirit soars with contentment, and you also know what it feels like when your spirit is wounded. Again, we all have our own unique methods for achieving spiritual adjustments. For some it is prayer, worship, or meditation. Others commune with nature to feel the presence of a power greater than themselves. Whatever you do, find a way to recognize and appreciate that you are part of something much greater than you can even imagine.

Some people outwardly seem to have everything, but if they are not feeding their souls—their spiritual selves—they will still feel empty. I believe it is really all about love. We are loved by God. We give love to one another out of gratitude for the love we receive. It's a continuous cycle. We constantly need to be loved and to give love. When we do it right and receive it right, we are spiritually growing. When we do it wrong and receive it other than the way it is intended, we suffer and crave healing.

I am a firm believer in setting goals, and I lead an action-oriented lifestyle of achievement. But I have found that when I chase after goals for personal satisfaction, I am less successful and less fulfilled. When I look up at the pattern, however, and see how my goals are instilled in me for the purpose of helping others, making connections, growing relationships, and deepening my faith, the pursuits of my life take on a new significance. I also find that with this mind-set, I am more clearly compelled toward these objectives and more likely to succeed. Off balance on purpose.

When we make space in our life patterns for the evolution of our spirits, we add a level of increased importance to all of our actions and interactions with others. With this heightened perspective, you will place more value on your work, your relationships, your health, and your personal interests. It is all connected in your life pattern. If you open yourself to the possibility that you are a spiritual being having a human experience, you will begin to notice amazing opportunities and connections that propel you down this path.

SPIRITUAL GROWTH SPHERE QUESTIONS

- How do you know that you are a spiritual being having a human experience?
- What new steps are you ready to take to grow along spiritual lines?

YOUR PERSONAL INTERESTS SPHERE

If you are like me, you will have no shortage of candidates for your personal interests sphere. For example, I really enjoy spending time with my wife and kids, playing golf, flying airplanes, reading novels, playing drums, watching movies, traveling, performing gymnastics, skydiving, and going on adventures. Additionally, I've developed an interest in learning Spanish, salsa dancing, taking a martial arts course, taking cooking classes, and studying yoga. I would also enjoy more time to practice my guitar. It is not challenging to come up with a list of things I would like to do. I suspect the same is true for you.

The challenge for you, then, lies in determining which of your interests are most important to you, and which are most congruent with your other four spheres. You can't do it all. Or, at least, you can't do it all at once.

It is important to pursue personal interests. This is how we relieve stress, define our uniqueness, acquire self-confidence, and expand our life experience. We also learn about ourselves, enhance our strengths, and challenge our weaknesses. This pattern includes our hobbies, reading, continuing education, recreation, journaling, and all of the items on our wish list of life goals and experiences.

Often, this is the area of your life that brings you tremendous satisfaction, because when you are pursuing your personal interests, you are doing what you enjoy the most. And when you are doing what you love to do, you feel alive and in touch with the person you really are—as well as with the person you wish to become. You bring the greatest value to the world by being true to your innermost passions and joys.

Unfortunately, this is also the area of your life that often takes a backseat to other influences. With all of the commitments of work and family, you cannot justify the time and energy to indulge your "selfish" desires. When you do steal away from the other responsibilities of life to enjoy one of your personal interests, you might find yourself burdened with guilt because of all of the other things you could or should be doing with that time. So, you are unable to effectively disengage from your work or relationship responsibilities to enjoy your free time, and as a result, you begin to resent your other responsibilities. Does this scenario sound familiar?

The solution to this dilemma is threefold. First, you need to validate that personal time is necessary and important in the creation of a healthy life. Remember, you are the one in control of the pattern. Your employer is not going to say: "Hey, you really need to take some time away from this project and go camping. How about you take tomorrow off and make it a long weekend?" It is up to you to be proactive in scheduling the time and energy to devote to your personal interests. Of course, it is important to keep your commitments. But in the long run, you will be most productive at work and at home when you are properly managing your life pattern, and this means renewing your spirit, mental health, and friendships by being true to yourself.

Second, prioritize your personal interests. Which are most important to you and vital to your life and renewal? Which activities are still enjoyable but less important to you? And, last, what are you doing now in your personal time that is no longer serving a useful or helpful purpose in your life? These are the items you should remove from your pattern to make room for the pursuits that matter most.

The third approach to managing this part of your pattern involves synthesis. Ask yourself, "How can I integrate my personal interests into my work, my relationships, my pursuit of better health, and my spiritual development?" As you have already seen (and will fully explore in the next chapter), it is the intersection of the different aspects of your life pattern that brings tremendous opportunities for fulfillment in your daily experience.

For me, these potential syntheses include enjoying shared interests with my spouse and friends (satisfying personal- and relationship-oriented objectives); playing golf with business associates (personal and work objectives); traveling with my family (personal/relationship); using my interests as material for my speeches and writing (personal/work); playing drums in the Praise Band at my church (personal/spiritual); and performing backflips and other physical stunts in my presentations (personal/work/health). By being creative and thoughtful, you can find new and exciting ways to bring your unique interests to all aspects of your life and all of your interactions.

PERSONAL INTERESTS SPHERE QUESTIONS

- What personal interests sustain and renew your spirit?
- How can you blend your personal interests into the other four spheres of your life pattern?
- What makes your life unique?
- What, potentially, is your greatest contribution to the world?

Pattern Fuel

Imagine your life pattern—five spheres in motion, tracing the path of an infinity sign and moving together in harmony. Got it? Good. What propels the pattern forward? Fuel. Like any fine-tuned machine, you need to supply the right kind of fuel in the proper amount to experience the best possible performance. Life pattern fuel comes in three types—money, energy, and time. Those three elements provide the push that keeps the spheres in motion and on course.

- *Money*—While your work sphere is the primary income generator, each sphere of your life requires funding. And the way you spend your money is a transparent reflection of what you value.

- *Energy*—This fuel source includes your physical energy and your mental energy. Remember, we have infinite potential for creativity. How do you invest your effort and your creativity? Here, your health sphere plays the primary role in fuel production.

- *Time*—What commitments do you make and keep? How do you move through your daily experience? Are you focused or distracted? Do you practice deliberate disengagement? Do you spend time complaining about how much time you don't have, or do you wisely wield the time you have?

As with all fuel consumption, you can easily find yourself wasting these resources or spending far more than required. Today, the consciousness of our society is shifting to value efficiency and to reuse resources in our industrialized economy. Increasingly, we are looking for opportunities to save energy, water, and environmental resources. This is a fantastic, positive shift in our culture and a trend that will certainly continue. We are beginning to understand the importance of the intelligent application of what we have and how to reuse (and recycle) resources without the need to re-create energy to satisfy new needs.

Similarly, as we manage our personal resources of money, energy, and time, we need to become more fuel efficient. We need to get better mileage. Think in terms of MPG—not "miles per gallon," but "maximum pattern growth." Spend your money, energy, and time in a way that contributes the best overall impact to your complete pattern.

Because your life is fully connected, every decision will impact every one of your life spheres. But how? It's time to answer that question as we now turn our attention to the key to your completeness, the uniting force within your life pattern: your lifelines.

7

LIFELINES: STRENGTHENING YOUR VITAL CONNECTIONS

INTUITIVELY, YOU KNOW that all aspects of your life are connected to one another. You recognize that when you have a stressful week at work or you experience health challenges or relationship issues, it affects your general mood and your approach to life. You aren't as present with your family and friends as you might like to be. These connections are part of our self-awareness. But have you ever really analyzed the nature of these connections? Probably not, and I don't blame you. The connections are so varied and ever changing, the task seems insurmountable. Mostly, you recognize the connections when things are beginning to spin out of control.

Many books that advocate "life balance" tell us we must be able to keep various aspects of our life separate from one another. We must prevent our work-related responsibilities from coloring the time we spend with our personal relationships. We need also to carve out specific time to devote to other important pursuits, such as improving our health, sustaining our spirit, or pursuing personal interests. Many authors and "experts" advocate a life that is compartmentalized, like the rooms of a house. Everything has its proper place.

If you have bought this idea, then I'm here to tell you that you have been sold a bill of goods that is only going to frustrate you and complicate your life. Life is fluid, and no aspect of it is ever static. Even when you think you have handled certain issues, you often realize that there is much more to address. Compartmentalizing our lives is not the answer. What we really need to do is integrate our life aspects in a new way. To do this, you need to understand and harness the full power of the pattern. You must inspect and improve the relationships among the spheres and your ability to assemble them in such a way that they are mutually supportive, healthy, and empowering.

With an understanding of your five spheres of influence—work, relationships, health, spiritual growth, and personal interests—you are now beginning to see your life pattern take shape. You understand that these five spheres are always in motion, responding to your input and decisions. Imagine how they move around the pattern, tracing the shape of the infinity sign and flowing harmoniously with one another. Part of what makes this possible is the connections among the spheres. When your relationships are strong, you have a better attitude and are more productive at work. When work is going well, it's easier to maintain good physical and mental health. And the connections go on.

I call these connections "lifelines."

The problem is that this unbroken, effortless state of spheres moving smoothly within the pattern, connected by strong, positive lifelines, is not the norm. What demands our attention every day are the spheres that fly off target, causing us to desperately attempt to catch them before they shatter or collide with other spheres and destroy the whole pattern. We notice the sphere collisions when our work schedule encroaches upon our relationships, inflicting tremendous stress. We notice our health when it is in jeopardy—when the lump is detected, the joint is sprained, or the irritating cough becomes chronic. When our relationships are threatened, we wonder how to fix them. When our spirits ache, we turn to our higher power.

But what if we could anticipate, prepare ourselves for, and easily correct breaks from the pattern? What if we could turn our attention to the inner workings of the connections among the spheres and make small adjustments that would improve all aspects of our life?

Only by understanding your lifelines and giving them attention can you anticipate pattern problems before they compound and become unmanageable. When you strengthen your lifelines with focused time, effort, and decisions, you also promote flexibility that will enable you to withstand unexpected challenges and maintain your resiliency and momentum.

There are ten lifelines, and they are all reciprocal in nature: in other words, changes you make and actions you take on one side of the line (to one sphere) affect the other side (another sphere) in some way—always. Repercussions are inescapable. There will always be some effect, and it will either be a positive or a negative result. But instead of waiting to see what those results are and responding to the consequences (trying to fix the messes we have made), we are going to start with the lifeline. We are going to explore the connections and strengthen them in powerful ways.

Because your spheres of influence are constantly moving within your life pattern, your lifelines are continuously being reshaped. At times, your lifelines will be obvious, strong, and completely reliable; at other times, they will be stretched to the limit. Our lifelines change over time, as spheres move through the pattern. But by giving the lines themselves attention, you strengthen them and make them more flexible, resilient, and dependable.

Your lifelines are the key to a fulfilling and rewarding life. Within them reside countless possible opportunities to recognize and remove the roots of your frustrations. Your lifelines will allow you to create new experiences

Lifelines Will Be Stretched, Contracted, and Tested as Your Life Pattern Changes Shape

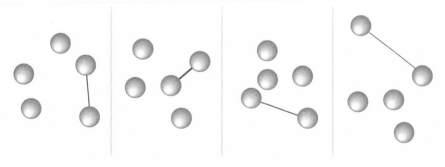

and make better choices that deliver the alignment and harmony you desperately crave. So wait no further. Let's explore them one at a time.

Lifeline One: Work ↔ Relationships

This lifeline is the one we think about most often. We place enormous pressure on ourselves, pondering the question: How do you have a successful career and a family or meaningful friendships at the same time? In fact, for many people this one question represents their entire thought process and concept of what "balance" is all about. It is tremendously important and complex, of course, but that question alone is an insufficient foundation from which to build a harmonious life.

The first thing to understand about all of the lifelines is that they are reciprocal. That means that, in this case, we need to think about the line that joins your work and relationships—this connection—from both directions. We will take this approach with each of the ten lifelines. It's a tall task, so let's get started.

How does your work impact your relationships? For starters, you earn money at work that enables you to provide for your family: pay for your home; put food on the table and clothes on the kids; provide health insurance; finance education, recreation, and vacation; and build a savings

account that will act as a buffer for unexpected expenses. That's quite a list, and it is no wonder that you feel stressed to take care of all of those needs. Providing for your family also provides a tremendous sense of purpose. Building a family and a life for your spouse and kids is an important mission. But what if there was more to it than just that? What else does your work bring to your relationships sphere? A lot.

If you have kids, your work provides an opportunity to teach your children what you do and why you do it. You can teach them vital lessons about business, service, ethics, and economics. You provide much more than a paycheck. Just think; you are a living example of what it means to make and honor commitments, to contribute to the world in a meaningful way, and to earn money because your efforts were needed. Work can provide travel opportunities for you and your family as well as new experiences and relationships that add texture, color, and flavor to your life.

In return, your relationships make you whole. Your family and close friendships and the love you share with them restore your strength and lift you up. Family teaches us that no matter what happens at work, we will still be loved. An audience member recently reminded me that dogs accomplish this same purpose. True, and I'm a huge dog lover (but the conversation leaves a little to be desired).

Work provides opportunities to grow new relationships. Not only do you deserve to produce enjoyable work that excites you, you should likewise enjoy the people you are around when you do it. When we work with people who become our friends, we are strengthening this lifeline. Spending time with the people you work with outside of the office, introducing them to your family, and deepening all of those connections also enhances the strength and flexibility of your number one lifeline.

Working with our family members is another option. I have worked with many remarkable family-owned businesses. In most cases, these companies maintain a close-knit community of employees that extends beyond just the family members. At their meetings I notice the entire organization is imbued with a well-defined culture, and that feeling adds a special character to the work experience and a stronger sense of purpose. Their people know it and value this fact. Regardless of your vocation, you can find creative ways to share work experiences with your loved ones. Along the way, you may create cherished memories.

> When my kids were younger, Sheilia and I frequently took them with us when I had to travel to speaking engagements. Before he was two years old, my son had taken forty flights! But with school commitments nowadays, that is increasingly harder to do. When travel is a part of your work experience, what can you do to ease the burden and strengthen the lifeline, even when it is stretched to the limit? Here's what I do.
>
> First of all, Eddie and Maggie both know exactly what I do and why I do it. My children understand the purpose behind my absence. They have both been to events with me and have even been on stage during my presentations. They understand the message I share with people and the reason it is important. They also understand that this is what pays our bills and provides the lifestyle they enjoy. But I also try to enlist their help and support for every program. At the exact moment when I take the stage, my family usually knows it, and they all say a "cheer" (part pep talk and part prayer) for me. I may not hear it, but I know it's happening. They honestly believe, as I do, that their thoughts contribute to the success of my program. They are part of the show even when they are a thousand miles away.
>
> I was packed and ready to go on another trip. Maggie came out of her playroom, flashing a triumphant smile and holding one of my juggling clubs in her hand. "Dad," she said, "use this one!" She turned the club and pointed the knob of the handle toward me, revealing a subtle, well-placed sticker—heart shaped and covered with sparkles. "Use this one, Dad. It has love on it," she said. I snatched her up, along with the club, and thanked her. Though I have dozens of juggling clubs, that particular one remains in my travel bag and I use it in every performance. After all, it has love on it.

Many more specific ways to strengthen this lifeline will be presented in the next chapters. For now, I want you to think about the opportunities and challenges that exist in your life, relative to your work–relationships lifeline. I know it's often difficult to choose how to spend your time. How do you keep all of your commitments? How do you finish all of the projects, spend time with your friends, attend the kids' soccer games, and romance your spouse? The answer lies in making decisions that are deliberate and purposeful—off balance on purpose. If, however, your work and your relationships are incompatible and constantly at odds, to the point that you are causing harm to your vital connections, it is time to find a new approach—or a new job.

TEN ACTIONS TO STRENGTHEN YOUR WORK–RELATIONSHIPS LIFELINE

1. Share the purpose and scope of your work with your loved ones. Explain the mission—why you do what you do.
2. Deepen your friendships at work. You don't have to like everyone, but find a colleague you can call a friend, and get to know her or him on a deeper level.
3. Introduce your family to your coworkers. Have dinner at your house for your boss or a close associate.
4. Have a "bring your kids to work day."
5. Ask your spouse for input about a business decision—and use it.
6. Employ your children to help you with aspects of an assignment. Teach them about the work and economics. Pay them for their assistance.
7. Demonstrate that your work supports your family but doesn't replace it. Purposely postpone an assignment—disengage from your work to engage in a meaningful moment with your spouse, child, or friend. You can't always do this, but show them you can, and do, put them at the top of the priority list.
8. Post pictures of your family and friends in your workplace.
9. If you travel, find creative ways to bring your friends and family "along for the ride." Travel together if it is possible, or remain in touch with phone calls or a Skype video call.
10. Form a Mastermind Group, that is, a friendly group of three to six peers whom you respect and can learn from. Meet on a monthly basis to discuss your opportunities to grow. Challenge one another to improve your skills, offer creative insights, and hold one another accountable.

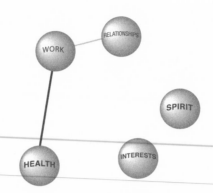

Lifeline Two: Work ↔ Health

Does your work support your health or place it in jeopardy? For many, sadly, the latter is the case. For millions of people every day, work equals stress, inaction, and bad food. This triple threat can lead to obesity, heart disease, pain, arthritis, and a really rotten quality of life. It doesn't have to be this way.

Why not make improving your health a vital aspect of your job? Instead of viewing those spheres as competitors for your time and energy, look at them together. See the connection, the lifeline, and ask, "How are these two spheres connected?"

I need to stay in shape to do my job. In turn, my job, to a large extent, keeps me in shape. The two go hand in hand. I'm over forty years old, but in "gymnast years," that's about ninety-seven! You just don't see many people my age willing and able to perform tumbling and acrobatics. Maybe that's why I do it. I fully intend to turn backflips twenty years from now. And I believe I will, if I can just stay flexible and healthy. This is my focus and daily discipline. I had someone say to me, "You don't really think you'll be able to do this when your sixty, do you?" My reply: "Sure. I just think it will be much more impressive."

You don't have to do backflips, but strengthening your work–health lifeline is a requirement for maintaining your life pattern. Whether you are self-employed or work for a company, the benefits to a healthier you are easily understood. For starters, improved health equals improved productivity, fewer sick days, and increased energy for vital tasks.

Remember from the last chapter that pursuing better health is simple (although not necessarily easy). It comes down to four things: what you put into your body, the amount of rest you give your body, how you move your body, and what you think. Along those lines, one of the most useful things you can do to improve health is to drink more water. Water helps your body eliminate harmful elements, promotes flexibility, keeps you cool, safeguards your organs, aids digestion, and gives you energy. Water makes up half of your body and 75 percent of muscle tissue. You simply cannot drink too much water, so always have a full bottle, glass, cup, or container within reach throughout your workday. Make this your number one habit and a constant reminder that you are oriented toward better health.

Look for opportunities to demonstrate to yourself and others your commitment to avoiding the pitfalls of a busy schedule. Become the person others seek to emulate. This may mean ordering the grilled chicken or salmon salad instead of the half-pound burger and fries when you head to lunch with your coworkers. Or it may mean adjusting your schedule so that you have time each day to tune up your thinking, exercise your creativity, or quiet your thoughts to dissipate stress. Because mental health is as critical as physical health, your attention to both aspects, and to the connection between the two, is equally important. You know the adjustments you need to make, so I won't tell you exactly what to do. But do it with pride, not anguish. Be bold when you assert your right to be healthy. Others will likely support your decision and choices. Then you become the model, providing positive influence for those around you.

When you engage in exercise by starting your day with a morning workout or walk, you may find profound benefits that carry into your workday. First you will stimulate your creative thinking through movement. As you pick up your heart rate, your mind will become focused, and potential solutions will occur to you when you least expect it, appearing to just pop into mind. You'll also feel better, starting your day with greater energy and the knowledge that you took action to improve yourself. Sure, you had to get up a bit earlier, but you are off balance on purpose (on your terms), and you feel great!

Even when you cannot make separate time for exercise or creative thought, you can integrate these aspects into your routine, creating a solid work–health connection. It truly is all about how you apply effort. Do you coast through the day, moving only when it is necessary and thinking only about those things demanding your attention? Or do you seek and embrace opportunities to apply physical and mental effort? Think in terms of expanding your range of motion and the scope of your intellectual engagement.

When you move, move with purpose. When you walk through the office, ascend a staircase, or reach down to pick up your pen or tie your shoe, be conscious of your physical movement. Feel yourself stretch, feel your muscles become engaged, and expand your range of motion. Similarly, when you think, think with purpose. Apply effort and focus to the mental challenge and stretch your thinking beyond its normal frame by asking new and better questions. The point is that there are opportunities in the course of our work endeavors to stretch ourselves both physically and mentally (and thus improve our health).

At the Atlanta airport, my home away from home, I often walk between concourses instead of taking the train. When I do ride the train, I grab the overhead handrail in order to stretch my shoulders. Instead of standing on the escalators and waiting for them to reach the next floor, I walk up them, secretly counting my steps to see how many I can take before reaching the top. (At the Atlanta airport, forty-five is about the limit before you start to look goofy.)

You get the idea. It takes effort and creativity, but not much, to turn your work life into a healthier experience. But as you do, you'll benefit not only from the physical rewards but also from the satisfaction of knowing you are improving a vital lifeline.

Good health is your birthright. You deserve to be healthy, so see yourself that way already—in the peak of physical condition. Don't let your lifestyle or work style interfere with the real, healthy you.

TEN ACTIONS TO STRENGTHEN YOUR WORK–HEALTH LIFELINE

1. Need a lift? Instead of riding the elevator, take the stairs.
2. Park as far from the building as you can, and enjoy a brisk walk to the office and back again.
3. Brown bag it—bring your own healthy lunch and snacks to work. This will save you some cash and give you control of your diet and your time.
4. Turn your lunch hour into a workout break. The time you will save by bringing in your own meal will afford you an exercise opportunity. Take a walk outside and enjoy the day, the activity, and some fresh air.
5. Stretch your thinking and your body. Take breaks throughout the day to reenergize. Stand up. Walk around. Stretch.
6. Go hands free with your office and mobile phone. It will help you improve your posture and avoid neck cramps. It will also give you the freedom to stand up and move while you converse.
7. If you travel, take advantage of hotel gyms, take a jog in an unfamiliar city, or use the privacy of your hotel room for exercise.
8. Become the example, not the tagalong.
9. Turn coffee breaks into water breaks. Stay hydrated and you will feel more energized and give your body its most essential ingredient for good health.
10. See yourself becoming more congruent every day, claiming the health and lifestyle that is your birthright.

Lifeline Three: Work ↔ Spiritual Growth

Chances are, if you aren't employed by a faith-based organization, you probably don't see your vocation as "spiritual." But it is. Or at least it could be. I believe that every job can be an opportunity for you to practice, hone, and act on your spiritual beliefs. In many ways, your job is the perfect testing ground for your spiritual growth.

Throughout your day, you have the opportunity to interact with many people, each of whom is in various states of distress or need. And, as you

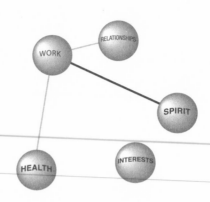

are in "business," you have products, services, or skills to help them address those needs and find solutions. That, in and of itself, is a wonderful purpose. Yet there is a deeper business to your interactions, and that lies in addressing and positively impacting at their core the people you work with and those you serve. I refer to this as touching their spirit. As you connect with people, you have a chance to reach them at a "soul level."

I don't mean that you should transform into the office prophet or begin wearing sandals and a robe to boardroom meetings. What I am talking about is a shift of focus, a change in intention that enables you to bring a calm and soothing demeanor (which is desperately needed) and a sense of love and compassion into your work environment. Don't tell people what you are up to—consider this a secret mission. Perform your job as it is required, but do it guided by principles, and watch how dramatically everything else changes for the better.

When you are bringing a spiritual approach to your job, you must follow more than your "office policy." You are guided by a code of conduct that includes honesty, humility, charity, compassion, ethics, and forgiveness. You are accountable, even when your actions could go undiscovered. You resist the temptation to join conversations that demean coworkers or customers. Gossip loses interest for you, and you pass it up easily. Instead, you become the person others can turn to with real concerns and issues. You provide a positive and understanding perspective. You give love, because it is all that you have to give.

As I write this, I recognize that living this model is an ongoing challenge, and we will never do it perfectly. That is the test—the spiritual test we all face.

The goal is spiritual growth, not divine perfection. You and I will fail every day to live up to these standards. But that doesn't mean we shouldn't try. When we falter, we realign our selves and our spirits and move forward doing the next right thing. Apologize when you offend or harm others, then forget it, look forward, and move on. There really is no place for guilt in a growing spirit.

Remember, we are talking about your spiritual growth, not your coworkers'. It isn't your place to hold other people responsible for their spiritual development. Concern yourself with your own, and you will provide a compelling example. Do the right thing for you, even if it means experiencing short-term setbacks or seemingly "unfair" repercussions.

Self-improvement is largely a process of "fake it till you make it." The same is true with improving our spiritual orientation. We are all, to some extent, making it up as we go along. But if you will act "as if" you are an evolving soul, you will be. And you may find that your work and business prosper better than they ever have before. A healthy life pattern not only greases the wheels of success but also enables you to enjoy it with a grateful heart.

TEN ACTIONS TO STRENGTHEN YOUR WORK–SPIRITUAL GROWTH LIFELINE

1. See your work as an opportunity to embody spiritual principles.
2. Meditate or pray to start the workday. Ask for guidance.
3. Understand the deeper purpose behind the work you do. Serve others not because you "have to" but because you "get to." It's a gift.
4. Be generous with your time and money. See the rewards of your prosperity create positive ripples throughout the world.
5. Dare to have deeper conversations with your closest coworkers. You don't have to evangelize (which may be inappropriate and annoying), but you can explore their thoughts about purpose and meaning.
6. Follow the Golden Rule—do onto others as you would have them do onto you—in all of your affairs.

7. Secretly, seek to influence others in positive and affirming ways. Smile, and make other people smile, as part of your job description.
8. Be peaceful, especially when others are not.
9. Politely remove yourself from negative conversations.
10. Pray for the people you work with and for—visualize their health and well-being, and bring those thoughts into your conversation with God or your daily meditations.

Lifeline Four: Work ↔ Personal Interests

When I learned to juggle, I uncovered something I was truly passionate about. I loved it. To me the practice hours would go by quickly when I was engaged in learning. I enjoyed the practice because it was fun and interesting, so it did not seem like a struggle. When you love what you do, the challenges become easier, and the rewards and accomplishments are so much more satisfying.

In those early years, as my practice turned into performance, there were some people in my life who thought this was surely a passing phase I would outgrow. But other people said to me: "Dan, I see what this means to you. It lights you up. Whatever you do, never let this out of your life." Those encouraging words from people I loved and respected never left me.

And to this day, performing, juggling, and many other personal passions remain a vital part of my work.

Do you love what you do? I believe that life is too short to work in a field that bores you. Your job is one of the most important and enduring expressions of who you are. For most of us, "work hours" represent the largest portion of our "waking hours." So why not approach your job with the attitude that you deserve to love it?

I'm not suggesting you quit your job and run off to become a world-renowned chef, lead adventure hikes in Peru, or start a rock band. Although that type of radical shift might be an appropriate and fulfilling path, you might also just try loving the job you have, whatever it is, and amplifying the aspects that bring you enjoyment and personal satisfaction.

Express yourself creatively. If your passion is creative writing, for example, you might pursue writing as a career. Or you could write an industry "blog," an office newsletter, creative proposals, persuasive letters and emails, and marketing copy. Use your talents and personal interests to reshape your job into something only you can do. Then you will become irreplaceable.

Your talents and passions are unique gifts. In order for your gifts to appreciate in value, it is not sufficient to appreciate your gifts. You must use them. Use them daily, and share your uniqueness with the world. When you can find the courage to do that, new possibilities will manifest that will surprise and delight you. Step into them willingly and see what happens next.

Work satisfaction also seems to be a requirement for high-level achievement. Choose someone you admire—anyone, from any field or industry—and I believe you will find one enduring trait. The successful, accomplished person is the person who derives personal joy, stimulation, and excitement from the work he or she does. Personal interest is an undeniable factor of success.

TEN ACTIONS TO STRENGTHEN YOUR WORK–PERSONAL INTEREST LIFELINE

1. Choose to work in a field and at a job that interests you.
2. Embrace the job you have now and throw yourself into your work wholeheartedly.

3. Specialize in the most engaging aspect of your job or industry.

4. Continue learning and growing in your job knowledge and skills. Develop expertise.

5. Bring aspects of your personality, hobbies, and personal interests into your work conversations—with coworkers, customers, and associates.

6. Organize events that combine your work and your interests, such as a golf outing, office book club, or football pool.

7. Return to your childhood. What fascinated you when you were young and caused you to lose track of time? Find ways to bring those interests into your work.

8. Transcend your "job description" and bring all of your talents to your position.

9. Sell your passion first and your product or service second. You may find that once you share your passion and excitement, your products sell themselves.

10. Live the dream you have been suppressing. Create a business or career that dares to be different, and sing your original song. When you are ready, follow the process outlined in part 3 of this book.

Lifeline Five: Relationships ↔ Health

Are you in "healthy relationships"? Are the most important people in your life encouragers of a healthy lifestyle, or are they saboteurs of your health-related goals?

Making changes in any area of life is difficult. When it comes to eating habits, exercise routines, and lifestyle changes, the challenge can be truly daunting. This is because we must reshape the very core of our behavior— how we nourish our bodies, how we seek comfort and rest, and how we move and challenge ourselves. It takes a new pattern of thinking to make these life adjustments. And the support (or discouragement) of the important people in our lives can play a huge part in our success (or failure).

You should surround yourself with people who support your goals and find at least one person who is an active supporter. One useful approach is to find a partner who will hold you accountable to your plans and promises. Ideally, your accountability partner should be someone you respect and admire, perhaps because they already embody the changes you're

considering. Or it could be a friend who shares your desire for change and wants to make those changes together. Be careful here. It can be extremely helpful to have a teammate, someone who shares your excitement for progress. But if this person has a history of failed attempts, or is unlikely to sustain the effort, their "best intentions" could be your undoing. For example, when the excitement and enthusiasm wear off and you are faced with a difficult choice, you and your partner may decide to let each other off the hook "just this once," infecting your relationship with enabling behaviors.

I believe in seeking a pro—someone who already has what you want. This could be a personal trainer or nutrition expert who you pay for guidance. Or it may be a friend who has already undergone the learning curve and survived the trials (stopped smoking, quit drinking, reformed eating habits, got in shape, or whatever the change is you are targeting for your own life). Their condition is solid and unshakable, so there is no "escape clause" in your commitment.

How will a healthier "you" impact your relationships? It is important to identify the purpose behind the changes relative to the vital relationships in your life. How will improved health make you a better husband or wife? A better parent? A better friend? What impact will you have upon the people you care about? By uncovering these answers, you will tap into a source of motivation to begin and sustain the effort. Making health improvements is not just about you. Your strides will enable you to enjoy better, more honest, more positive, more fulfilling, and more intimate relationships with the people you truly care about. The biggest benefit is that you will have more energy to share with them and to devote to building and improving those relationships.

It is not about trying to change others ("I'll quit smoking, but only if you lose twenty pounds"). This is about making your own changes in a more supportive and effective way. Ask for help and support, but don't expect others to follow suit. As you begin to improve your health sphere, you will be setting a powerful example for the people you hope to influence—your spouse, your kids, and your friends. Let those actions (and results) speak for themselves, and watch the positive ripple effects.

But you must also be prepared for the likelihood that you have "friends" who will try to stop you from improving your health. They will unconsciously seek to sabotage your efforts because your changes cause them discomfort. Your improvements force them to question their own choices and behaviors, and that makes them uneasy and conflicted. This may mean people you considered close will suddenly distance themselves from you. Or it could mean that you need to create the separation yourself. Be true to your desire to improve. It comes from a deep sense of purpose. Ultimately, honoring your inner voice, and following through with sustained commitment, is the greatest way to influence the people you care about.

TEN ACTIONS TO STRENGTHEN YOUR RELATIONSHIPS–HEALTH LIFELINE

1. Share your health-related goals with the people closest to you and ask for support.
2. Plan exercise excursions (hikes, walks, games, yoga classes, etc.) with a partner who shares your interest and desire.
3. Get physical with your kids. Join their games and take the "family time" outside for a romp in the grass or a toss of the football (instead of surfing TV channels sitting on the couch together).
4. Find an experienced workout buddy and make a plan to push each other toward your goals.
5. Participate in a walk-a-thon fundraiser (for a cause that you support) with family or friends.

6. Throw a healthy potluck supper, inviting friends to bring their best-tasting healthy dish and to share recipes.

7. Instead of "doing lunch" at a restaurant, have a healthy break with a friend or business associates. Take a walk together and bring a healthy picnic lunch you can enjoy.

8. Distance yourself from the people who sabotage your health progress. Surround yourself with people who will support your growth.

9. Seek a support group of people who have made the changes you desire. Find out how they did it and harness the power of their experience.

10. Enjoy laughter (and the unparalleled health benefits it releases) with your loved ones. Find ways to laugh together, frequently.

Lifeline Six: Relationships ↔ Spiritual Growth

Just as our relationships can support or undermine our health goals, they also have a direct impact upon our spiritual growth. All of the same concepts apply. We have friends who share our desire to grow along spiritual lines and others who dismiss it as unimportant or become threatened by our intentions. Some people will serve as guides toward enlightenment, while others offer detours.

If you believe in God (whatever your religious persuasion), you also must know that we are all in this together—the saints (whoever they are) and the sinners (the rest of us). We are all connected, joined by the loving force that is God—the source of power that flows through all things.

Our relationships are the point of contact where our beliefs meet our actions. In other words, the way we relate to the people in our lives is an expression of where we are in our spiritual evolution. How you treat others—family, friends, strangers, and even antagonists—is the living demonstration of your spiritual progress.

Call it a test if you like, or a blessing. Either way, the challenging people in our life are our opportunity to practice spiritual principles. Regardless of the circumstances and justifications, we have a mandate to be loving, forgiving, kind, and compassionate, even when that is the hardest thing for us to do.

When I began to realize progress in the area of spiritual growth, I wondered if some of my friendships would be threatened. But ultimately, all of my important relationships improved. I became a better husband, son, and friend. I was confronted by my shortcomings and found myself aware of changes I needed to make. Of course, I resisted this at first. But God is patient and persistent. I eventually began to accept the changes that were required of my lifestyle and of my heart. While I will never live a "perfect life," the attempt to improve and approach a higher standard pays enormous rewards.

For me, having children has been the single most powerful example of where my relationships meet my spiritual growth. In fact, becoming a father was a pivotal moment in my spiritual evolution. When my first child was born, and I held him in my arms, I was transformed by the force of his presence. Although Eddie was only eight pounds, the weight and magnitude of the moment was enormous. Instantly, I had a new understanding about love—unconditional love. While I had experienced love before—the love of my wife, my family, and my friends—this was entirely different. This love was greater and more pure than anything I had previously felt or contemplated, and it was (and continues to be) a divine gift.

Loving my children as I do, without limit or hesitation, allows me to better grasp what God's love is all about. And I know that the love I experience as a father still falls short of the love this higher power feels for me, for you, and for all of us. Regardless of what we have done in the past, this limitless love is available to us right now and forever.

Every relationship offers endless opportunities for us to be enlightened because relationships—all of them—are challenging, at least at some point. They present ethical challenges, moral challenges, ideological challenges, and more. Our relationships test us daily. And they offer daily opportunities to interact in a loving and spiritual manner. When we don't live up to the challenge, we know immediately by the way we feel—regret, sorrow, loneliness.

But the missed opportunities are harder to catch. They slip by unnoticed. Maybe it's the opportunity to make somebody feel better, to right a wrong, or to offer encouragement. Regardless, we have to be vigilant, because those are the opportunities that will bring us closer to enlightenment. There are endless opportunities to grow, to interact in a loving and spiritual manner, and to move you along on your journey toward a satisfied soul, and those endless opportunities are all unique.

TEN ACTIONS TO STRENGTHEN YOUR RELATIONSHIPS–SPIRITUAL GROWTH LIFELINE

1. Love the people in your life who cause you grief and difficulty. Recognize that they may be imperfect (as are you), but they are also spiritual beings having a human experience.
2. Apologize for your mistakes as quickly as possible. Ask for forgiveness, and remedy any damage you may have caused.
3. Find a spiritual mentor, someone who has the type of peaceful relationship with a higher power that you desire. Get to know this person and begin to model their thoughts and behaviors.
4. Get involved with a small group of people to discuss or practice spiritual principles and develop friendships. This may be a church group, or it may be another type of gathering. Find a place where you feel comfortable, challenged, and stimulated to grow spiritually.

5. Perform community outreach by working at a homeless shelter, visiting a nursing home, building a Habitat for Humanity house, writing letters to prisoners, picking up trash, or any number of other options. Pick one, and join a team of people who share your desire to take action. Bring your family and friends with you, or build new relationships along the way.

6. Perform spontaneous loving deeds without taking any credit (or even telling anyone what you did).

7. Pray or meditate for spiritual guidance before you have tough conversations with the people in your life. When you do, you'll find yourself less focused on expressing what you think is justified and more loving and empathetic, and you'll be amazed at the results of those encounters.

8. Sponsor a child in a foreign country. There are many organizations that can facilitate an opportunity for you to connect with a needy child and contribute a small dollar amount per month that will have an enormous impact. You can also communicate with this person and make them an extended part of your family.

9. Forgive someone who hurt you, even if they may never ask for forgiveness.

10. Pray or meditate with your family—at suppertime, at bedtime, in times of need, or at any time you feel inspired or grateful.

Lifeline Seven:
Relationships ↔ Personal Interests

How do you spend time with the people in your life? This lifeline is about exploring shared interests together and supporting the pursuit of passionate learning.

There are limitless choices for life adventures, distractions, and courses of learning. Some things we decide to do because we think they would be fun, others because we feel we are obligated, and some (the golden few) because we must—we are absolutely passionate about these interests and are off balance on purpose. When you uncover an interest that is so central to your being, you have discovered a gift that must be acknowledged and embraced. Don't let it out of your life. The question to ask yourself, relative to this lifeline, is, "How can I share my passion(s) with my family and friends?"

Equally important is that you are able to support and encourage the personal quests of the people in your life. But because of life's obligations and activities, we sometimes subjugate our own interests to make concessions for others, to handle urgent matters, or to assume responsibility for something. That sacrifice can be admirable, and it can be one technique for strengthening this lifeline. But to make this the norm—abstaining from your passion, your undeniable expression of life—will only foster long-term frustration and resentment. To improve your alignment, find a way to incorporate your vital personal interests into your relationships.

This doesn't mean that your spouse has to be just as jazzed about the subject as you are. But it does mean this gives you a great opportunity to express this aspect of who you are and find out what is equally meaningful to your life partner. Then you can find a way to support and encourage one another. Perhaps you and your spouse (or family member or friend) can develop an interest, or at least an appreciation, for one another's passions.

We have very few interests that fall into the "must" category, and they are truly gifts. But life offers countless opportunities for learning and experiences that would be enjoyable or interesting. Pick some—they are waiting for you! In conversations with your family and friends, discover the interests you share, and make a commitment to pursue them as partners. Plan an excursion, take a class, or make a date for one activity to get the ball rolling. Then follow through.

Today there is more to learn and to experience than ever before. The secrets of the universe are no longer secrets. They are answers, available and at your fingertips. You can know or do anything your imagination conjures. So embrace life in earnest, and share the experience with the people you care about. Express your interests. Encourage theirs. Celebrate passion wherever you see it.

TEN ACTIONS TO STRENGTHEN YOUR RELATIONSHIPS–PERSONAL INTERESTS LIFELINE

1. Share your desires, dreams, interests, and aspirations with the people you cherish. Ask them to share theirs with you.
2. Validate the interests you (and your loved ones) must pursue, as they are an undeniable gift, an expression of who you (and they) are.
3. Identify the shared interests you enjoy, or might enjoy together.
4. Sign up for a class with your significant other or a friend. Choose an activity (cooking, dancing, tennis, painting, astronomy, auto mechanics, or whatever) that both of you are enthusiastic about, and enjoy the journey of learning together.
5. Coach your kid's/kids' sports team/teams. Get involved in your kid's/kids' interests and activities.
6. Support your significant other's interests, even if they aren't yours. Give him or her the freedom to passionately pursue them without feeling guilt or obligation.
7. Become a cheerleader and celebrate the successes of your friends and family, and offer encouragement from the sidelines.
8. Take a trip with your loved ones to a place that offers interest, learning opportunities, and shared enjoyment.
9. Develop friendships with those who share your interests. Expand your circles, your connections, and your perspective.
10. Join (or start) a book club.

Lifeline Eight: Health ↔ Spiritual Growth

What is the connection between your physical health and your spiritual well-being? Does God really care if you are in shape? Doesn't the higher

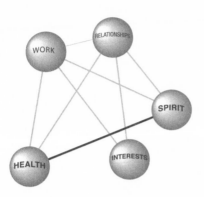

power have better things to do than count our calories or make sure we do our sit-ups?

Improving your health is a parallel pursuit to spiritual growth. The two are inextricably linked in a number of ways. Some believe that a person's physical health is a tangible manifestation of that person's spiritual health. Spiritual well-being or discord changes our physical form as well as our experience. And our mental and emotional health is directly tied to our spiritual health.

In the Bible, Corinthians 6:19–20 tells us, "Your body is your temple," and these five words have been used by parents, priests, and promoters to advocate everything from abstinence to abdominal workout videos. That verse has been interpreted to mean you should keep your temple free from contaminants and clutter. For others, it carries the meaning that we should adorn and decorate our temples with jewelry, tattoos, and piercings.

Your temple, your body, is the place where you spend every second of your earthly existence. For me, therefore, it follows that the form you inhabit is your training ground, your classroom, your place of study, your special project, and your outward expression of your inward condition.

It comes down to your thinking. When you consider your physical condition, do you think health and perfection or do you think illness, lack, and fear? It's impossible to overstate the power that your thinking wields over your state of health. It is everything. Your thoughts can heal you or make you ill. Sounds like a pretty easy choice. Yet, without a spiritual footing, how could anyone maintain the belief of physical perfection or possibly feel that he or she deserves perpetual health? The connections among your spirit, your thinking, and your health are the essence of this lifeline.

Your thinking alone has enormous consequences, but your thinking also drives your actions. Your health is something you can and do influence every day with every choice you make—how you eat, how you move, how you celebrate, how you relax, how you think, and how you worship.

We all face or will face challenges to our health. Our temples are built for one owner, designed to wear out and yield to time. But even those advanced years can be experienced gracefully if we establish a lifelong reverence for our bodies and choose wisely the methods for our sustenance and recovery.

TEN ACTIONS TO STRENGTHEN YOUR HEALTH–SPIRITUAL GROWTH LIFELINE

1. Eat for nourishment, not as recreation or entertainment.
2. Make your exercise an act of worship. Whether you are running on a treadmill (or on a street), doing aerobics classes, practicing yoga, or simply taking a walk, make that time your spiritual time of reflection and prayer.
3. Skip a meal (or several). Fasting is a time-tested spiritual practice. When you forgo your habitual meals (while still taking in plenty of water, juices, or nutrients, depending on your fasting plan), you will go through some physical tests and changes. These tests and changes are challenging, which becomes a chance to pray for guidance and strength. In this way, when you are less dependent on physical nourishment you become more reliant on God. And fasting can also be a wonderful way to cleanse your system. Start with a meal or two and progress to longer fasts only if you are in good health. Follow a safe and predetermined plan.
4. Listen to spiritual speakers and teachers, or read spiritual messages before, during, or after your exercise times.
5. Manage your attitude toward better health. Do not fight illness. Embrace and welcome health. Use your physical condition as a testing ground to demonstrate the power of your thoughts and prayers.
6. Exercise with people who share or stretch your spiritual beliefs.
7. Avoid overindulgence, remembering "all things in moderation."

8. Help meet the needs of others who are sick and hurting. Minister to those who have a lack of health, and share your health abundance.
9. Push past the level of what is comfortable, physically and spiritually. You must overtax your present ability in order to grow.
10. Be the transformation you are pursuing, today.

Lifeline Nine:
Health ↔ Personal Interests

There are countless ways you can get a workout. Pick one that interests you. For example, I don't enjoy running. I never have. It takes too long and inflicts too much stress on my knees. Biking is more fun for me. To really peak my interests and get a great workout quickly, I take a five-mile, thirty-minute unicycle ride up and down the Georgia hills where I live. That's my thing. I love it.

What method of fitness is most suited to your interests? Experiment, and find one you truly enjoy. The workout itself will become one of your interests, especially when you start to see results.

You can take this same approach to foster your mental health. Choose stimulating activities, such as crossword or Sudoku puzzles, to get your brain in gear. Read challenging material about subjects that interest you. Research the topics you are curious about, and develop your expertise.

Remember that a huge part of mental health involves releasing stress. Practice your passions as a means to shed your mental burdens and experience relief from taxing circumstances.

Develop an interest in nutrition and healthy eating. The more you know, the easier it will be to make wholesome choices.

TEN ACTIONS TO STRENGTHEN YOUR HEALTH–PERSONAL INTERESTS LIFELINE

1. When you move your body, plug in your brain. Listen to a book (or your favorite music) to make the workout time more interesting.
2. Subscribe to Consumer Reports on Health (www.consumerreportsonhealth.com), a monthly publication that highlights the latest facts and tidbits about health and fitness—and debunks the latest myths. It is a quick read, and you will always find at least one thing that is interesting and useful. This publication is unbiased and accepts no funding from any outside business, group, or association.
3. Learn to cook for yourself in a way that is both tasty and healthy.
4. Try a different workout every week, and notice how various forms of movement and exercise affect your body.
5. Pick one type of exercise that you really enjoy. Become a devoted student—learn as much as you can about it, and make it a regular part of your life.
6. Take a walk in a beautiful or interesting place, such as a nearby park or (when you travel) an unfamiliar city. Look around and enjoy the surroundings as you get your blood pumping.
7. Plant a garden. Not only is this a physical activity, but it will also provide fresh produce for your table.
8. Enroll in a dance class—salsa, swing, or whatever groove that moves you. You'll have so much fun you'll never even notice you are burning calories.
9. Do some physical work to give back to your community—build a Habitat for Humanity house, clean up a community, or stock a kitchen for charitable giving.
10. Set a personal goal that involves physical activities, such as climbing a mountain trail, biking a formidable distance, or some other physical test. Set this goal in a location that you have always wanted to visit. Then begin training as you work toward your goal.

Lifeline Ten:
Spiritual Growth ↔ Personal Interests

Spiritual growth requires an interest in spirituality. Getting this "spiritual being thing" is not a matter of something you "have to" do. It is a "want to" endeavor. True spiritual growth comes about when you become passionate, craving with your heart and soul an intimate connection to the divine in and around you. And, when you are engaged in this pursuit, you will be undertaking the most important (and interesting) journey of your lifetime.

But we all come from unique backgrounds and perspectives. We each have our own story. So the way we accomplish spiritual growth—prayer, church involvement, faith, belief, worship, service, love, devotion, and teachings—is a complex and personal endeavor. My spiritual path will be different from yours.

We all find spiritual questions and answers in the context of our personal experience. For example, those with obsessions often find their higher power through the pain of addiction and the process of recovery. It usually takes a "breaking point" discovery that self-centered living is impossible or at least unbearable. Only then does an interest in something beyond one's self develop, and a person seeks to rely upon some other source of direction,

guidance, and healing. Some people seek spiritual growth because of an event that rocks their world—an unexpected setback or an unexplained miracle. Most of us, however, have some level of interest that ebbs and flows depending on life events. Progress, if there is progress, is slow and uncertain.

Spiritual growth is a full-time gig—a daily discipline. Otherwise, you are idling back and forth and getting nowhere. So, the key to this lifeline is to first get interested in growing spiritually and then to find and enhance the connections between your existing personal interests and your spiritual growth.

We have been members at two churches in the past ten years. In both places, I've played drums and accessory percussion with the band. For me, that is the best way to experience worship—through music. Drumming has been a lifelong hobby for me. I haven't the talent or inclination to be a professional drummer, but I'm good enough to participate and contribute a little something to our service. It has been a great way for me to become more involved in our church, to develop relationships, and to experience spiritual growth. Sheilia belongs to a group of women who regularly perform community service and meaningful works. That is her interest, her passion—putting faith into action and making a tangible difference in people's lives.

How about you? What is the path to spiritual growth that excites your interest?

TEN ACTIONS TO STRENGTHEN YOUR SPIRITUAL GROWTH–PERSONAL INTERESTS LIFELINE

1. Consider the proposition that your spiritual growth is the whole reason why you are here. Your personal events and circumstances provide the context for you to learn, grow, and love.
2. Get involved with an organization by sharing your interests and talents.
3. Join a study group and develop a deeper understanding of your faith, whatever it is.
4. Find opportunities to get involved in your community by doing interesting, meaningful work for others.

5. Volunteer financial support to charitable causes you are passionately interested in. There are so many ways to "give back," so pick one you are passionate about, and make a meaningful difference.

6. Go on a mission trip to a part of the country (or world) you have never visited.

7. Read something at the start of each day to further your spiritual interests. There are many books that provide a short spiritual message for every day on the calendar. Choose one. Even just two minutes can make a huge difference in your perspective and growth.

8. Keep a journal. Pour out your thoughts and feelings on paper (or keyboard). Improving your intrapersonal (self) communication will help your thoughts become more clear and honest, and it is good for the soul.

9. Learn a method of meditation.

10. Attend a spiritual retreat somewhere interesting. Commune with nature as you communicate with God.

As you can plainly see, the choices for developing and strengthening your lifelines are limitless, just like your personal potential. By tapping into this powerful force, you will bring your five spheres into a better, more sustainable, and more fulfilling pattern. You will move through your days more willing to create and accept new challenges and opportunities. And you will begin to recognize the connections between your pursuits and your aspirations. These connections bring meaning to the madness, enabling you to embrace an off balance life in a purposeful way.

8

COLLISION AVOIDANCE AND RECOVERY

January 10, 2005. Fraser Cain writes in *Universe Today* that NASA's Spitzer Space Telescope has spied a large collection of dusty debris (about the mass of our Moon) near Vega, the fifth brightest star in the night sky, located approximately 25 light years from Earth. The theory, presented to the American Astronomical Society in San Diego, is that this field of particles represents the aftermath of a planetary collision between objects perhaps the size of Pluto. Astronomers believe the young planets collided and then continued to smash into smaller and smaller particles, creating the smaller-than-sand-grains debris that was observed by Spitzer.

January 10, 2008. Astronomers believe they have found evidence 170 light years away of a collision between planets about the size of Saturn and Uranus. National Geographic News reports that the planet is "unusually hot" but not as bright as the heat would indicate. The theory is that lingering heat is an aftereffect of the planetary crash, which occurred perhaps a hundred thousand years ago.

October 26, 2028. An asteroid (about a mile wide) will come close to colliding with Earth, passing only thirty thousand miles away. (Quick aside:

On July 1, 1998 the film *Armageddon* was released, depicting a doomsday scenario when a Texas-sized asteroid is noticed only eighteen days before it will crash into Earth. Bruce Willis leads a team of deep-core drillers who become reluctant astronaut-heroes who must land on, then blow up, the giant rock.) Should the real-life asteroid's course change slightly in fall 2028, its impact upon colliding with Earth would have the force of 2 million atomic bombs, according to Jack Hills, Los Alamos National Laboratory scientist. Bruce Willis will be seventy-three years old by then. Good thing we have more than eighteen days' notice.

IN THE PAST two chapters, I have presented a model of your five life spheres—work, relationships, health, spiritual growth, and personal interests—moving and growing in a healthy relationship with one another. In the best of times, with the right decisions and proper guidance, your life spheres flow together with symphonic motion, each fueling the others to maintain a positive course and take on greater dimensions and possibilities.

But what happens when the respective movements of our spheres are not in sync with one another? How does this manifest in our real-life experiences, and what do we do about it?

When Spheres Collide

At this point, you can likely envision a healthy life pattern—that is, one in which your spheres maintain their optimal paths, speeds, spacing, and relationships. If any one of those five spheres is impacted in a way that alters its course (torpedoed by a massive asteroid, for example), it may change its path and its position relative to the other spheres. Initially, however, the alteration will be very subtle. In fact, it may be unnoticeable for quite some time. In the end, though, the deviation will become more pronounced. The path becomes noticeably different and wobbly. The positive tension—the lifelines—that once kept everything in order begins to shift. Some lifelines begin to snap, eventually bringing the spheres onto a collision course with one another. By the time you realize what is happening, it is too late to avoid the impending crash.

Our spheres of influence are never static. They are influenced by outside forces and by the effects of time and attraction. We can surely expect to find them, at times, on collision courses, where competing demands or objectives promote an inevitable conflict. We may not notice when our spheres first shift out of alignment with the pattern, with our purpose. Nevertheless, the events and disruptions at long last will be too obvious to overlook.

When the spheres of your life pattern collide, they will create chaos and debris—just like the planetary collisions I described at the beginning of the chapter. Explosive, emotional energy is released, generating intense and uncomfortable "heat." In the aftermath of the explosion, confusion sets in as we try to figure out "What just happened?" Perhaps you have experienced this personally. Maybe you find yourself in the midst of a dust cloud right now. These devastating moments can be the catalysts for growth, understanding, and personal evolution. Or, if you don't investigate and properly understand them, they can be just another in a series of unfortunate, unpleasant events.

When spheres collide, lifelines are shattered, and this creates the sense that everything is falling apart. In a sense, it is. Your lifelines are the infrastructure of your world, the cohesive ties that enable stability, flexibility, and options. When you break a lifeline, you become unstable and inflexible, and you find that your options have become limited.

This chapter will help you recognize and avoid most of the collisions before they happen and make adjustments that will prevent catastrophes.

Early detection of the shifts and misalignments is the key. But sometimes, those collisions are unavoidable. And when they do happen, lifelines need to be mended and restored. Consequently, I'll also give you some useful ways to promote healing "after the crash."

Smashed Spheres

Joe is a real go-getter and really wants to provide the best for his family. So, he buckles down and works long hours, leaving early and arriving home late, exhausted from the day's demands. This pattern of action creates a rift between Joe and his family, who don't understand the work obsession that consumes him. Joe's wife becomes bored and begins to dream of finding affection elsewhere. Joe returns home one Friday to the news that his kids are out of the house, staying with his wife's parents. BAM! Joe's wife then tells him that she is tired of this life and is filing for divorce.

Bill smokes, and he has for the better part of his adult life. Sure, he knows it's bad for him, but it's just "who he is." And, he seems to be able to smoke with impunity: he rarely gets sick, and he is able to maintain a busy and productive schedule. Life is good. He tries not to smoke around his young kids, but they know he smokes. They can smell it on him, and they hate that. Bill is going to quit . . . one of these days. Then he goes to see his doctor for a routine checkup, and the visit swiftly becomes a life-changing event. BAM! Bill has lung cancer.

Jane is a busy person, and she thrives on getting stuff done. Because of that, she is the "go-to gal" anytime someone needs a project completed. She volunteers for everything—church committees, school activities for her kids, neighborhood projects, charitable causes, you name it. What she doesn't realize is that in her effort to be all things to all people, she is losing her ability to distinguish her own sense of direction. She has become a puppet for the whims of other people in her life, but she doesn't even realize that until . . . BAM! Jane wakes up one day and finds herself on the edge of a nervous breakdown, resentful of the obligations that consume her, overwhelmed by the tasks on her overflowing plate, and unsure of how she got here or where she's going.

When your spheres are out of alignment with your life pattern, you may be able to compensate to keep things moving. Maybe you sleep a little less. Perhaps you make excuses and promises to your family to explain why this is just a temporary condition. You cope with the taxing demands on your body, mind, relationships, and spirit . . . for a while. Eventually, however, you will reach a breaking point when it becomes too much to bear. Either you'll recognize the jeopardy you face, or the circumstances of your life—the paths of your spheres—will produce an event that will profoundly get your attention. At that moment, when the spheres of your life crash into each other, you will be forced to change course.

Early Detection

I want you to avoid life's catastrophic collisions before they happen. That's why I wrote this book—so you can understand the inner workings of your life pattern and what is at stake. The fact that you are reading this proves you have already taken steps toward early detection. The awareness you have developed will change your thinking about the choices and actions you make and take. But let's take it a step further. What specific things can you do—what systems can you put into place—that will help you recognize and remove potential collisions before they happen? Here are a few.

IDENTIFY AND REMOVE WHAT DOESN'T FIT

When something doesn't fit in your life pattern and poses a threat to the harmony and smooth movement of your spheres, it merits concern and action. Sometimes the remedy involves making some small adjustments that allow you to integrate various aspects in new, more beneficial ways. But there are some items that jeopardize everything, yet offer no purposeful benefit. Or, in gentler terms, they compromise what matters most to you without offering anything in return.

> Alcohol had been part of my life since my college days. I suppose that is normal, to an extent. But as the years after graduation rolled on, I continued to

consume alcohol with gusto. Eventually, I realized that it was beginning to consume me. It appeared I was not immune to the alcoholic tendencies that run in my family. For me, drinking is a complicated and ingrained behavior. And when alcohol was part of the scene, it became my central theme.

I recognized that alcohol didn't make anything in my life better; in fact, it only seemed to jeopardize the other things I cared about. So I asked, "Where does it fit in my life pattern?" and honestly answered that alcohol wasn't part of my work sphere, it didn't better my relationships, nor did it improve my health. And drinking is a poor substitute for a spiritual experience. In fact, my affection for alcohol could only harm and undermine every one of those four essential areas of my life. By a process of elimination, I concluded that drinking could be classified merely as a "personal interest," a twisted hobby of sorts. I was good at it, but my proficiency did not help my life. Instead, it presented conflicts, contradictions, and concerns.

As my career as a motivational speaker and author was taking off, so was my drinking habit. This contradiction made me feel deceptive and unworthy of the success I was enjoying. I knew that to persist on that path would lead me to a collision of spheres that would have catastrophic consequences. I could not get any better or continue to grow toward my potential as long as I kept drinking. I would never be a better husband, father, friend, speaker, writer, or citizen. Instead, things could only get worse, and if I were unwilling to alter the trajectory of events, in the end I would become just another tragic story.

So, with effort and guidance, I removed alcohol from my pattern. Today, every area of my life is better because of that decision. I am so grateful to have been able to avert a collision, and I remain ever mindful of my vulnerabilities.

Take a moment to think about this question: what one thing—habit, commitment, obligation, relationship, or responsibility—if removed from your life pattern, would have the greatest overall benefit to the quality and harmony of your life? Chances are, the answer comes to you quickly. We have a natural instinct for these things. We know the answer, although it may be unspoken. Speak it. Voice your intentions, and make a commitment to follow through with action. If something doesn't fit with your success plan, or your other spheres, it is your obligation to remove it. That doesn't mean it will be easy. It may be incredibly challenging, uncomfortable, and intimidating. Do it anyway, because it will ultimately be worth all of the effort. When you do, it is the equivalent of upgrading every aspect, each vital sphere of your pattern.

If you are unsure of the answer, ask yourself what you think is holding you back. What are you trying to achieve, or what activities are you engaged in, that cause extreme conflict? Measure the anxiety you are presently experiencing against the real or potential benefit to your five spheres and the question "Does this fit?" will be answered.

CALIBRATE YOUR INSTRUMENTS

Seismologists (scientists who study earthquakes) use sophisticated instruments to measure earth tremors. They can detect the subtlest movements and provide advanced warning about impending destruction, but only if those instruments are properly calibrated. Calibration is the process of confirming the accuracy of the observation—comparing what is perceived to what actually is. The purpose of calibration is to eliminate "bias" in an instrument's reading.

When we are asked to observe and evaluate our own life situation, it is not easy to eliminate bias (or another version of it, bs). After all, we are so close to the subject matter (us) and so emotionally connected to the events (our lives) that we will naturally default to a state where we might get faulty readings.

Imagine stepping on the bathroom scale to see how much you weigh. The pointer spins clockwise to rest on a number that makes you pretty comfortable. You're feeling good—until you step off the scale and notice the pointer has spun back to rest five pounds to the left of zero. Looks like you've allowed a little bs to creep into your measurement.

What can you do to reduce or eliminate the bs readings in your life observations? Well, you need to reset your scale to zero, to calibrate your instruments on a regular basis. Here are a few ways to do just that.

Form an Accountability Group
Some call this a Mastermind Group (which I mentioned earlier in the context of strengthening your work-relationships lifeline). This is a small

number of peers (three to six is usually ideal) who meet regularly for the purpose of providing feedback and guidance to one another regarding life issues. It is NOT a social club where you share complaints and get kind but unhelpful "buy in" to your assumptions and woe-is-me perspective. This is a place for action, accountability, and challenging conversations. There are many resources available to help you form and manage a Mastermind Group. Some basic tips include:

- *Mutual respect*—While it can be helpful to have members from different perspectives and areas of expertise, you should ensure that everyone has something valuable to contribute as well as a desire to grow, learn, and turn ideas into action.

- *Mandatory meetings*—This is another reason to keep the number of members small. You want to schedule meetings so that everyone will attend. No-shows are unacceptable as they drain the spirit of the team.

- *Goal-oriented members*—There is no point in belonging to a Mastermind Group if you are completely content with your life. Group members should have clearly defined goals and objectives to bring to the discussion.

- *Focused agendas*—Begin every meeting with a plan of attack. Members should know ahead of time what they are there to discuss or do, and they should come prepared. Choose a leader for each meeting to keep the group focused on the agenda.

- *Positive intentions*—Although injecting "devil's advocate" comments is a healthy part of the discussion, the spirit of membership should remain positive and encouraging.

Establish "Reference Standards"

Another means for gaining accurate feedback about your life is to establish unequivocal standards to measure and pursue. There are some things that are simply undeniable. For instance, it is more difficult to inject bs when you are working with numbers or standards, as the following points illustrate:

- If you are working on a financial goal, your standard might be eliminating a specific amount of debt, achieving a target net income, adhering to a predetermined budget, or generating a specific amount of revenue.

- If you are trying to reduce your weight, choose a number, set incremental steps to reach it, and measure regularly (with an accurately calibrated scale).

- To get in better shape, establish a specific workout routine, such as a walking/jogging route, a specific amount of time on the exercise bike, or a pattern of exercises with specific numbers of repetitions. Because the routine remains consistent, you'll be able to notice your progress as the challenge becomes easier.

- Set standards for your spiritual growth, such as a certain amount of time spent daily in study or prayer. Even a five-minute reflection at a certain time of day will help you mark and track your progress.

- Do the same with your personal interests. It was only when I started keeping accurate scores at golf (playing by all of the rules) that I was able to determine my actual skill level. As I continue to record my scores and stats, I know whether I am improving or not. It's not guesswork.

- What is your standard for maintaining a healthy relationship? Is it going out on a date a certain number of times per month? Spending a regular, specific amount of time with your kids? Keeping a regular get-together with a friend? The answers will be different, of course, for every person and relationship.

Perform Periodic Adjustments

Over time, you'll begin to notice that the patterns you have in place just aren't working like they once did. It takes regularly scheduled maintenance (and even an occasional complete overhaul) to keep you on a growth track.

When your Mastermind Group isn't providing the same value, you might need to change the schedule, the approach, or even some of the members.

Your standards for excellence will drift over time. Because of your improvement, what used to be challenges might be cakewalks, and you need to raise the bar. Or, you might see the opposite trend. You used to be able to devote a certain amount of time to a pursuit, but because of a shift in life events (a new child, a new job, or simply new priorities) those old standards are no longer useful. Make those adjustments consciously. Otherwise, you'll feel that you are falling short of what you "should be doing," and you'll burden yourself with unnecessary guilt.

Don't stop dreaming. Engage in active thought and goal setting on a regular basis. Continue to expand your vision for what is possible in your life. You will never be fully engaged simply trying to maintain your present situation. That is only an exercise in frustration, as your present situation is a snapshot in time. Always visualize new attractive possibilities for your future.

Reducing the Clutter

When I was a kid I was hooked on Asteroids. You know, the video game. After school I would fill my pockets with quarters (tip money from my neighborhood paper route) and stroll down the street and across Pulaski Avenue to the 7-Eleven, where my nemesis resided. In case you don't know it, the object of the game is to command a miniature spaceship (stunningly represented with an outline of a white triangle) and steer through an asteroid field (white outlines of rocks) without colliding with them or getting shot by the occasional alien spacecraft.

What you had to do to survive Asteroids was to blast the drifting rocks with your laser guns. When you hit a large asteroid, it would explode into additional smaller asteroids, further cluttering your path. But if you continued to shoot the smaller ones, they would continue to divide until, when you blasted the smallest rocks, they would vanish from the screen and provide a wonderful sense of accomplishment. That is, until you completely cleared the asteroid field and reached the next level—faster and more complicated.

Asteroids illustrates very effectively the challenges we face in life. Our path is cluttered, for sure—distractions, opportunities that aren't aligned with our purpose, the minutia of our daily lives. As we've already discussed, our task is to maintain our focus on the pattern, get rid of foreign bodies, and detect and handle impending collisions as early as possible, before it is too late. But the clutter in our lives makes early detection difficult. And when we "attack" a large project, we find that it "explodes" into lots of smaller ones. Initial efforts to make things better inevitably create more chaos and multiplied problems. And just when you think you have it all handled, when you have cleared your screen completely, it quickly resets with a more daunting set of challenges. You have reached the next level.

It's like the superhero Mr. Incredible says in the wonderful film *The Incredibles*: "I just saved the world. Can't it stay saved for awhile?" Nope.

So the question and challenge for all of us is how we reduce life's clutter on an ongoing basis. The clutter makes it hard to see the pattern, hard to find our way through the field, and hard to see the possible collisions on the horizon. There are different types of clutter, and, equally so, there are simple things you can do to diminish their negative impact on your life.

PHYSICAL CLUTTER

We live in a society that accumulates. We are assaulted by advertising, television programming, and people who convey the message that having the next great "thing" will bring us the joy we desire. After all, isn't that what money is for—to buy more stuff? I am as guilty of this as anyone. But time and time again, I discover that the purchase of anything brings an obligation as well as an opportunity—a new learning curve, time commitment, or sense of responsibility. These are the factors that are left out of the advertising. At the heart of our desire (and the promise of most sales copy) is a life that is simplified. Obviously, such a life will not be accomplished through accumulation.

You have too much stuff, and the solution is really pretty simple. Get rid of it! Streamline your life. There are different approaches to this challenge. You can organize a garage sale, or you can catalogue and inventory all of your extra stuff, list each item on eBay, host multiple auctions, and monitor their progress. Then package and ship each item to the "winner," provide feedback about your purchasers, and hope they will do the same for you, so that your eBay rating reflects that you are a "certified stuff provider."

Maybe you detect a note of cynicism there. It was only partially intended. The thing is, both approaches—and many others like them—

are the equivalent of smashing big rocks (I have too much stuff) into little ones (let's do a million other things to address this one big thing). Wouldn't giving it away be a simpler and more effective prospect? There are many organizations that will happily take your stuff, free of charge, and rid your life of some clutter with relative ease on your part. Plus, when you give, you will always receive something far more valuable in return. Life is like that—it is impossible to give more than you receive.

That said, if one of the issues that you are struggling with is money (one of our pattern fuels), then selling some of your items can help in this area. And you might decide that something you once enjoyed no longer fits in your pattern (it has become clutter), and selling it might provide resources you can devote to the new things in your pattern. I encourage you to think about this in terms of big-ticket items. Don't waste a lot of time trying to sell something for five dollars (unless, of course, one of your passions is to barter or to go antiquing).

MENTAL CLUTTER

Have you ever had the experience of lying awake in bed, exhausted but unable to sleep? While your body is lying perfectly still, giving a convincing impression of rest, inside your head you were running marathons, turning backflips, and negotiating cruel and complicated obstacle courses of your own design. A busy brain is a side effect of a busy life. The problem is that it may be difficult to turn off (or even down).

How you spend your thoughts is how you spend your time. What you think about, as we have already discussed, becomes amplified and abundant in your life, attracting more such thoughts and tangible results. This is why it is of supreme importance that you take an active role in policing the traffic in your cerebrum. You must strictly enforce regulations about what is and what is not allowed to dominate your mind. Because, when you are slack about this task, the default of your thinking is all too often negative representations that will do you harm.

These brain killers include: worry, indecision, procrastination, obsession, regret, guilt, and avoidance of responsibility. Taken in one gulp, this is quite a list, isn't it? These emotionally charged words no doubt made an impact on you, as they each correspond to real-life issues and dilemmas you have faced or are confronting now. But what makes the list interesting to me is that although these forces wield such enormous power in altering our life experience, they are, upon logical examination, completely inert. When you move in for a closer inspection, you see them for what they truly are, and—like a child who is frightened of the nighttime monster on his bedroom wall until he discovers it is only a funny shadow cast by his nightlight—you can reclaim your power over imagined impending disaster.

Worry is uncertainty about what might happen. You can control some elements about the future, but others you cannot. Instead of fretting about the unknown, handle what you can and then show up to see what happens. Instead of projecting disaster, expect resolution. The unexpected may be better than you dare to dream.

Regret and guilt are just two forms of worry, in this case, about what has happened. It's in the past. Get over it. Move on.

Indecision, procrastination, and avoidance all affect what needs to happen but which is not happening—*because of you*. You need to take action, because that's what life is all about, particularly if you want to grow. So,

- Let go of negative representations.
- Write down the things that need to happen, or write why you are indecisive about or are avoiding a certain action.
- Make a decision.
- Take action upon that decision.
- Practice meditation to quiet your mind and reclaim control of your thinking.

THE CLUTTER OF ACTIVITY

Like many parents, my wife and I have over-programmed our kids in our desire to provide exposure to well-rounded learning opportunities. We are passing along our twisted notion that more activity and more commitments always lead to a better life. This simply isn't the case.

> Eddie and I were riding our bikes in our neighborhood when he asked me, "Dad, can we do this every Friday?"
>
> "I'd like to do this as much as we can. Let's try to take a bike ride together every week. But it doesn't have to be on Friday."
>
> "But Dad, Friday is my only free day. Monday and Wednesday I go to Tae Kwon Do. Tuesday I have piano lessons and Cub Scouts. Thursday is soccer, and we have games on Saturday. And church is on Sunday."
>
> So much for a carefree youth!

Not only do we have too much stuff in our lives, we may have too many commitments. The difference is, you can't pick up the phone, call the Salvation Army, and ask them to drive a truck to your house and pick up a garage full of commitments you would like to donate. Commitments are "sticky," and you may find it difficult to release them from your grip.

Why? Perhaps it is because others depend upon you. And if you don't do it, then who will? But part of this equation involves our own feeling of worthiness. It is part of our identity: We are because we do. We are because we are needed.

I'd be willing to bet there is something in your life, an existing commitment, an unhealthy relationship, or an obligation that you can release. While the initial act of un-committing may be uncomfortable, the net effect will be positive and liberating. So what's stopping you?

When you liberate yourself from one commitment (and even if you do not), another "opportunity" will quickly present itself, and you will be tested. What will you say? Here's an idea; how about "No thank you." When you decline, please follow these guidelines:

- *Say "no" conclusively*—Don't be ambiguous with your answer, saying, "I'll have to think about it" or "Let me check my schedule." Say, "No. I'm sorry, but I'm not available." This conveys that your schedule will not accommodate another commitment at this time.

- *Say "no" politely*—Be direct, but do not be rude. There are plenty of nice ways to decline an invitation.

- *Say "no" with gratitude*—It is a special thing to receive an offer to participate. It means that the other people involved value your skills and abilities or interacting with you. Acknowledge that, and thank them for the opportunity. Then say no.

- *Say "no" without excuses*—The less talking you do to justify your response, the better. Keep it simple and resist the temptation to explain just how busy you are and all of the reasons why you can't do it. Once they get the answer, they need to move on, and so should you.

- *Say "no" confidently*—You are sure you are making the right decision and response. You are also confident that they will find "the right person" for the job. You are also confident that it is not you.

It may seem odd in a book about engaging life that I'm telling you to refuse opportunities. It's not a blanket statement. I want you to be involved, engaged, connected, and in action. But in order to be "on purpose," you must know how to select the choices that are right for you and decline (or deliberately disengage from) the tasks and obligations that will only take you farther away from your goals and the path toward your infinite potential.

If you are to live off balance on purpose and in better alignment with your purpose and pattern, then saying "no" is a skill you must master. Practice it today, and notice the rush of freedom you feel when you protect your time and take control of the direction of your life.

When Collisions Are Unavoidable

I believe that certain events in our lives—explosive encounters and devastating detours—are unavoidable. As you read this, you will likely think of one or several such circumstances that have happened or are happening to you. Despite your best efforts, determination, and careful planning, a comet of change solidly strikes your foundation and shakes the footholds you depended upon for structure and certainty. Cars crash, homes burn down, people get sick, couples divorce, and people lose jobs: All of these come to mind as examples of the comets that could potentially collide with our lives. But even less dramatic events can have an overwhelming impact on any one of us, especially if we never saw it coming.

If I were to say that such things are "necessary," you might find the statement to be hollow or even insulting, especially if you are in the midst of an ordeal at the moment. But it is not a casual comment; I truly mean it. Sometimes collisions are turning points, opportunities to redirect the courses of our lives. The positive aspect of a negative circumstance may not be apparent immediately, or even for a long time afterward. Yet it is always there. Everything happens for a reason. I believe that there is a divine plan in the works and that we are participants in ways we cannot always understand. Time brings the clarity we initially find so elusive.

So, how do you recover from these events, turn the tragedies into triumphs, and transform into the person you are meant to become? The final part of this book will provide a road map. This section is about how you can repair the pattern of your five spheres when they collide and shatter the ten vital lifelines that provide the structure that supports you. It is up to you to master damage control.

Mending Lifelines

It's collisions in the five spheres that get your attention. Need some examples?

- *Work*—You lose your job. You get transferred to a new city. You receive a "promotion" that offers the same compensation and twice the workload. You get caught in the midst of a legal or ethical scandal. You start your own business and fail or experience an all-consuming, runaway success.

- *Relationships*—Marriages or long-term relationships end. Friendships are compromised, abused, or betrayed. Kids make rotten choices and end up in trouble.

- *Health*—Accidents happen. Illness interrupts the best of plans. When our health demands center stage, it can often be a showstopper.

- *Spiritual growth*—Desperate moments cause us to search for meaning. You do some soul searching to examine your faith and realize you don't have any. After all, purpose is, in part, a spiritual thing. If you don't feel it, perhaps your spiritual relationship is unsteady.

- *Personal interests*—True passion and talent are often relegated to the back burner so that you can handle "real life." But as time passes, you may realize that your opportunities to become a master of what you truly love have slipped by. You're left wondering "what if?" and feeling that you've missed the whole point of your life's journey.

These are huge events, or at least you would perceive them that way should they happen to you. But as enormous as these occurrences might be, the response that will set you back on track is probably a small but significant action. You don't recover by fixing the spheres. You begin with the lifelines. When your world is shattered, it's the infrastructure of your life that needs attention. Start with a framework of choices and actions to restore a healthy and stable foundation on which you can build. Then you can move forward with confidence. When your lifelines are strong and flexible again, your pattern will be restored.

Let me share the story of a dear friend of ours who recently went through an unexpected divorce to illustrate what I mean. While this was clearly a devastating and challenging time for her, it ultimately proved to be an opportunity for a personal transformation that was remarkable and inspiring to witness.

Initially, the damage she faced was extensive, impacting every sphere of her life pattern. The first steps involved controlling the most important factors: Finding a new home, providing guidance and stability for her children, securing a new job (she was previously employed with her spouse), and getting support from friends and family. She refused to blame circumstances or speak ill of her spouse; instead, she focused on her responsibility for her life and the next steps. She deepened her faith throughout the process, asking God for guidance and comfort. She received them both.

With this "fresh start" perspective, she was able to revisit some personal interests and passions she had long suppressed and to seek out work opportunities related to those interests and her faith. Today, she is embarking on a new business of her creation, one that is tremendously exciting and stimulating. And through it all, she continues to be an inspiring example to those who know her, especially to her kids.

STEPS FOR MENDING LIFELINES

1. Address the wreckage and handle the immediate circumstances. Do damage control.
2. Take responsibility for your role in the situation. Identify the choices you made that led to this undesirable outcome. Or, if it is something that happened to you unexpectedly, take responsibility for what happens next.
3. Apologize for your missteps if those decisions resulted in negative consequences for others. Be humble and open to new ideas and input.
4. Slow down and simplify the next steps.
5. Make a new choice that will ultimately repair the connection in your life. Transformation begins with a single, simple decision combined with action.

When spheres collide and lifelines are broken, life becomes more difficult for a time. But these events tend to get your attention and make you willing where you were previously reluctant to learn or grow. Then you can become the architect of an improved design for your life—one that allows you to expand all your spheres in unison. We will never be successful at avoiding every bump in the road, but we can learn to recover more quickly and make choices that bring multiplied rewards.

9

SUPERCHARGED CHOICES YIELD
MULTIPLIED REWARDS

IT'S DECISION TIME. All eyes are upon you. Which way will you go? What path will you take? It's your call, and the impact of your choice can forever shape your life, for better or worse. Time's up, so let's have it. What is your decision?

Every day, life presents you with myriad choices in all shapes and sizes. Some are relatively simple, such as how you like your eggs, what you wear, or what you will watch on TV. But interspersed with these innocuous quizzes are real-life puzzlers. We encounter questions that demand answers, and sometimes we are unable or unwilling to conjure a definitive and confident response.

- "Should I take that job, even if it means moving to a new city?"
- "Can I make it if I try to start my own business?"
- "Is this the person I'm supposed to be with for the rest of my life?"
- "Is the time right to have kids?"
- "Paper or plastic?"

This chapter is about decisions—what they mean, and how we can make them with greater ease and confidence. As you read this, contemplate your real-time life issues. What decisions are presently on your plate? Whatever they are—as mammoth as a new mission or as straightforward as a new pair of slacks—you can decide with certainty if you take two steps. First, assess the decision in terms of your five spheres; this is particularly important for bigger decisions. Second, develop a process that helps you determine how to choose, what to choose, and how to know whether you made the right choice.

Step One: Assess the Decision in Terms of Your Five Spheres

When you invest your money, energy, and time, make sure that the decision has the greatest positive impact possible upon your life. In other words, make supercharged choices. A supercharged choice is one that simultaneously elevates two or more of your life spheres. This is fairly easy to do, since your spheres are so interconnected by lifelines. Get creative, and find a way to use your pattern fuel (time, energy, and money) to simultaneously benefit two, three, four, or all five spheres at once.

Challenge yourself to find or invent activities and opportunities that accomplish this objective. When you do, you will experience greater growth, better alignment with your purpose, and the satisfaction of investing your resources for a gigantic return. Plus, it's fun to exercise your creativity and integrate the most important aspects of your life.

I believe the real key to making decisions that will bring you into better alignment and enhance your life experience is to think multidimensionally, with your ten lifelines in mind. A decision and its resulting path become far more exciting and purposeful when they strengthen several (or all) of your lifelines at once. Because your choices and actions have pattern-wide repercussions, it is vitally important that you make your decisions from as wide a perspective as possible. By expanding your view to encompass all of your spheres, and by understanding the pattern of the internal relationships among the spheres, you insure against costly mistakes based on "tunnel vision."

Tunnel vision results when we are predisposed to a certain outcome. We decide in advance that we want to have a certain experience, purchase something we "must have," or avoid a difficult conversation with someone in our lives. Narrow thinking often explains why we make poor decisions relative to our work, our relationships, our health, our spiritual growth, and our personal interests. Tunnel vision impacts what we consume, how we indulge ourselves, and how we use our resources of time, money and energy.

When you cultivate an expanded awareness, you are confronted by the impact of your decisions and actions upon all of your spheres. Like any new routine, this initially will seem awkward, challenging, and slow. But with practice, it becomes the "new normal"—the standard process you will trust and implement as you navigate your life's journey. It becomes easy and fun to employ your pattern perspective as you see the immediate impact it has upon your confidence, fulfillment, and creativity.

A SUPERCHARGED CHOICE MAY LEAD TO A LIFE-CHANGING ADVENTURE

The key is not to say "yes" to a choice or life experience simply because it seems like a good idea or satisfies one of your life spheres. Find multiple reasons to say "yes" and experience the power of multiplied rewards.

One of my most important supercharged choices was deciding to travel to the Middle East to entertain and motivate our troops.

I was standing on a stage in Fort Lauderdale, Florida, preparing for a speech still two hours away, when my cell phone interrupted my routine. I answered, and the first five words I heard both chilled and excited me. "Dan, this is the call. We're leaving on March 6, traveling to Afghanistan, Iraq, Kyrgyzstan, Uzbekistan, Qatar, and Kuwait. We will do twenty shows in twenty-five days to entertain the troops. Are you in?"

The question caught me off guard. True, I had been waiting for "the call" for a long time. To perform for the brave men and women of our military had long been an important personal goal. But to leave right away for nearly a month? What a disruption to my family responsibilities, my business, my commitments to my clients, and my obligation to write my first book. The timing was all wrong.

I had just two days to make a decision, and my family and I discussed it at length, sharing both our excitement and our concerns. In the end, we decided that the purpose outweighed the risks. Our inconvenience and sacrifice were small compared to the commitments of thousands of men and women in our Armed Forces and their families. After all, if they could part for a year to serve our country and perform difficult, dangerous jobs, then I could certainly accept a far less dangerous assignment for a fraction of that time. Together, we decided this was a once-in-a-lifetime opportunity, something I needed to do. I approached the decision, as well as the "mission," with a multisphere mentality, knowing that this could be one of the most supercharged choices of my life.

- *Work*—I expected the trip to provide a number of stories to share with future audiences, and I knew it would enhance my life experience and offer new perspectives to strengthen my speeches. I did have to reschedule two bookings—something I had never done before—but I was able to make that a win-win client experience by increasing my commitment to my client—delivering an expanded version of my program and including additional "bonuses" for attendees. The organizers, sponsors, and participants understood the special circumstances and felt that they became partners in the success of the tour. Also during the adventure, I kept an online journal and shared the journey with interested clients and members of our database. When I returned, the presentations I made for the two "partner" clients, as well as many others, were very powerful and moving.

- *Relationships*—Although sacrifices would be involved, we decided that in the long run, my relationships with my wife and kids would be strengthened by the experience. The bond that was forged among all of the traveling/performing companions made us a "brotherhood" of sorts that we will always treasure. And, unexpectedly, during my time in Iraq I met a man from my hometown—Marine Major Ron Tootle—who has since become one of my best friends.

- *Health*—There were some obvious concerns about my health and safety, of course, because I would be in dangerous territory. But there was no way to avoid that reality. As it turned out, we ate well to sustain our energy, and kept up a regular workout regime from base to base. And even though we slept sporadically (averaging just four hours per night during the first week) and traveled constantly, I ended the journey feeling fit and energized. Plus, the exposure to so many new ideas kept our minds constantly stimulated.

- *Spiritual growth*—My family and I decided to view my month away as a retreat of sorts, a time of prayer and reflection. All of the performers would give their best efforts without monetary gain, simply out of a desire to serve. I would also have the chance to attend church services with military personnel in the Middle East. (On Easter Sunday, in Al Quaim, Iraq, for example, we worshipped in an old railroad car that had been converted into a chapel and nicknamed "The Soul Train.")

- *Personal interests*—The downtime on flights and between performances afforded chances to read books and magazines. I was also able to focus on practicing my juggling skills and expanding my interest in other areas. For instance, I learned from my fellow performers how to perform tricks with a six-foot bullwhip, I took many photographs, and I shot video footage to document the trip. The entertainers also took advantage of the generosity of our hosts, touring bases and learning volumes about military operations, technology, and culture. It was a fascinating education, forever changing the way I look at the news and enhancing my appreciation for the brave men and women of the U.S. Army, Air Force, Marine Corps, and Navy.

The timing for these performances would never be exactly "right." Going into a war zone to entertain this audience was certainly an off balance decision. But I did it on purpose—deliberately, and for many important reasons. And because of that, it was a supercharged choice that yielded multiplied rewards. I returned a better person for the experience, with all of my lifelines strengthened and the rewards multiplied through all of the spheres of my life. And I would do it again in a second.

What supercharged choices have you already made? And as you examine your life today, ask yourself where you might already be engaged in a single activity that delivers multiplied rewards. Recognize how this approach is already working for you. What new choices would catapult your life spheres to new heights? The possibilities are endless. Just as you will never reach your full potential, you will never exhaust the options for striking new, stimulating combinations.

SELFISHNESS VS. SELF-FULFILLMENT

You don't have to visit a war zone to feel the same sense of purpose. You can squeeze more juice out of whatever life experience you find yourself in, and you can reap a new and greater satisfaction in your day-to-day decisions. But first you have to decide that you deserve it. Some would call that a selfish viewpoint. The counterargument goes like this: "Why should I seek more out of life when there are so many other people in desperate circumstances? My life is what my life is, and I should accept it, deal with it, and move on." Maybe. Maybe not.

What if you are actually capable of much more than you realize? What if you truly have an infinite capacity to learn, grow, and love? What if making an off balance decision can actually bring you greater purpose than you have ever dreamed? Asking these types of questions and revealing honest answers to them will lead you not to selfishness but to self-fulfillment.

Self-sacrifice is admirable and necessary in order to grow. We all have responsibilities to uphold and obligations to fulfill. But you also have unique gifts and talents. You have dreams that are yet uncovered. You cannot diminish your innermost desires and still provide the greatest gifts to others. To achieve "complete success," you really need to address both aspects. As you do, maintain your alignment, but make bold choices—not for one reason but for multiple reasons. Then you'll realize the multiplied rewards life has to offer you.

Step Two: Develop a Decision-Making Process

Life choices are opportunities for you to artfully shape your life pattern and strengthen your lifelines. But it's also helpful to have a process that you can practice to make purposeful decisions each and every day. And the way to make and live your decisions is off balance on purpose: deliberately, thoughtfully, with conviction, and with a complete investment of yourself. You need to be "all in."

HOW TO CHOOSE

The first part of the decision-making process is to determine exactly how to choose what's best or right. While every decision presents its own unique qualities, the following factors constitute an effective, empowering approach that can be applied to all of your decisions:

- *Consciously*—We cannot avoid making decisions. First, decide to decide. An inability to decide is itself a choice—one that relinquishes control of your life to other people or outside circumstances. The trouble is, you might not like what you end up getting, and by the time you know it, your alternative options may be slim or nonexistent.

- *Knowledgeably*—Start by checking your premise. Be informed. Does this really matter to you? Why? What is your motive? Answer those questions, and then learn all you can about available options and the necessary details.

- *Purposefully*—Get clear about what you value and what you believe. Solid principles simplify decisions.

- *Multidimensionally*—With life's big decisions (and even some small ones), you need to get the big picture. What impact will your choice have on all five spheres of your life—that is, your work, your relationships, your health, your spiritual growth, and your personal interests? There are no "isolated" choices.

- *Completely*—Commit to your decision 100 percent, without an escape plan or mandated "requirements." It's like renting a car and driving out of the parking lot. When you pass the security gate and cross over the speed bump with one-way metal spikes, you'd better keep moving forward. Backing up will only result in "severe tire damage." So put it in gear and go!

WHAT TO CHOOSE

The second part of the decision-making process is to determine exactly what to choose. The following factors will help you in your selection:

- *Easy over difficult*—Do not battle your choices or brace yourself for conflict. It's not necessary. Smart decisions (even the big ones) should be easy, as long as you ask the right questions and start from a solid foundation. The right choice, because it is a new path, may be challenging. But the decision is easy.

- *Simple over complicated*—Get down to the basics. What is the real issue—the main thing about the main thing? Don't turn this into a mental obstacle course. Keep it simple.

- *Gut over head*—Once you have gathered sufficient information, follow your instincts. Most decisions are made with the gut and then rationalized afterward. And that is not a bad thing. Betray your gut, and you might end up with puke on your shirt.

- *Evidence over wishful thinking*—Past results and actions are real indicators of possible outcomes. Especially where people are concerned, the evidence of past behaviors is difficult to dispute or "wish away" in the hope for a different outcome tomorrow.

- *Positive over negative*—Every thought you have and each response you make is an opportunity to choose a positive or a negative path. Choose positive. This isn't an altruistic, lip-glossed view of what is best for the planet. This is vital and what is best for you! Negative thoughts and actions always induce conflict, stress, and anxiety. Positive thoughts and actions empower you and enable positive results, more often than not. So be nice. Be inquisitive. Be excited about abundant opportunities—not irritated by limited options.

HOW TO KNOW WHETHER YOU MADE THE RIGHT CHOICE

If you ask this question, you haven't really made a choice. You still have one foot on the other (untaken) path. Life is too short for "split decisions."

Choose, and move forward. How do you know it was the right choice? You made it. It was right for that moment, decided for the right reasons. Everything happens for a reason.

When you know yourself, and you operate from that secure mental footing, then choices become opportunities to test and demonstrate your purpose. They become easier to make as well, because you are not simply rolling the dice and hoping for the best.

The OBOP Process for Having It All

Living off balance on purpose is a repeatable process that contains five steps. As we move into the last part of the book, I will use the acronym OBOP (pronounced "Oh-Bop") to describe the method for applying these ideas to your life circumstances. The steps are:

1. Own your reality

2. Seek your purpose

3. Lean forward (and make yourself uncomfortable)

4. Leverage your resources

5. Follow through

Each of the five chapters in part 3 that follows will focus on one of these steps. As you progress through them, you will learn to use this process for two extremely important reasons.

One, it will help you formulate a plan for your life and modify and improve that plan moving forward. Now that you understand the concept of the life pattern and how the spheres are connected within it, you need to figure out what your life pattern actually looks like. To get the "big picture," you need to take these steps with that perspective in mind. You will be asking and answering larger life questions. The result will be greater clarity about your present situation, your purpose, and your future plan of action. From time to time, you will reassess these overarching questions and repeat the process.

Two, it will help you take purposeful daily action. As your familiarity with the process improves, you will be able to quickly apply it to specific situations every day. You will learn to assess your circumstances at any given moment, decide what you want (and why you want it), use your available resources, and follow through with action.

By adopting an off balance on purpose orientation to your life, you will experience internal rewards: less stress and better health as well as greater joy, meaning, and purpose. Happily, this means you will also reap external rewards: achievements and accomplishments both personally and professionally. I truly believe that you can have it all, and that you owe it to yourself to be a complete success.

To some people, success is a reflection of how much money they earn. To others, success is all about how much they are able to help other people. Still others measure success by their social status or by maintaining a certain state of health or fitness.

The success I am talking about, though, is multidimensional. It is a state of being. A complete success spans the five spheres: work, relationships, health, spiritual growth, and personal interests. These are all wrapped up into one exquisite work of art called "your life." For you this means transcending the ordinary, making creative choices, and achieving breakthroughs. And it's not just in this or that area; it's right across the board. To do this, you have to look up, just like an expert juggler does, and see the big picture.

Remember, life isn't just sitting there, posing quietly while you study it from all angles. It is fluid, constantly shifting and changing, all-encompassing. We cannot pursue happiness by focusing exclusively on one or two of the five spheres. True satisfaction and life enjoyment can come only from making forward progress in all of these areas. It's a question of alignment. If you feel as though you are pursuing a number of disjointed, unrelated objectives simultaneously, you will quickly find those objectives at odds with one another, and you'll become overwhelmed. The only way to find peace and contentment in your life is to see that all of your goals are interrelated, all taking you to the same place. Hold on to the vision of your life as a pattern of simultaneous pursuits, with each of your spheres moving in mutually supportive harmony with the others.

Some people have a problem with the idea of "having it all." They identify with the struggle and see it as a way to define themselves and validate their importance. They feel that life is meant to be an arduous journey fraught with disappointment, failure, and sacrifice. As I discussed earlier, there certainly is a "gift to the grind" (and those times of struggle are usually necessary and blessed life moments), but you should likewise enjoy the journey. See past the immediate obstacles to identify positive and ever-expanding possibilities.

You deserve to be happy and healthy. Your life is supposed to be satisfying. You possess extraordinary gifts that demand to be used and shared with the world. Don't deny your destiny. Taking control of the direction of your life can be intimidating, especially when you are unsure of which direction to travel. Don't worry, the third, final part of this book will help you find your inner compass and strike out confidently toward your destination.

Part Three

THE OBOP PROCESS OF SELF-EXPANSION

10

OWN YOUR REALITY

THE INTERNET ERA offers us instant global communications and immediate answers to life's tough questions. Borders between nations are becoming blurred, and even remote regions have access to and are members of an increasingly aware and empowered citizenry. When future generations look back at these years, what will be the historical reference point for our present-day world? Energy and environmental consciousness? Philanthropy? The entrepreneurial spirit? My guess: reality television.

This genre of programming has existed in some form or another since the start of the medium (remember Allen Funt's *Candid Camera*), but beginning in 2000, it has become a staple of American and European culture. Producers are riding the wave of popularity and inventing new ways to thrust average (or exceptional) people who want a shot at fame into an unfamiliar situation so that a nation of voyeurs can second-guess their decisions from the safety of our sofas.

The biggest complaint about reality television is, ironically, that it isn't "real" enough. After all, what real-life situation involves voting competitors off of an island, dating two-dozen women at once, or trying to swallow live insects without vomiting?

Nevertheless, these situations are interesting to us because we are riveted by the "truth" of how real people act when presented with an undeniable, unambiguous predicament. Life presents us with so many "fuzzy" scenarios and open-ended questions; it's refreshing to watch what others do when facing clear challenges, no matter how contrived the circumstances.

As we enter into the final part of this book and learn a process for self-expansion and growth, it is my earnest desire to help you clarify your choices and illuminate the path that will lead you to greater purpose and joy in your daily life. And the "reality drama" that unfolds in your life every day is far more interesting and important than anything you will see on TV.

Just as beauty is in the eye of the beholder, "reality" is defined by the participant. What you choose to observe, focus on, and determine about your life is exactly what you will experience and share with others. There is not one reality but endless "versions," each determined by the viewpoints, agendas, opinions, values, and interpretations of the participants at any given moment. The problem is, we are so close to the subject matter (our lives) that we begin to adopt our view as gospel. We look for validation and find it in observational evidence to support our case and willing witnesses who testify in our defense.

But what if your assessment of reality is totally off? What if you are basing all of your efforts and energy on a false premise—a mistaken measurement?

This chapter will help you comprehend your real-life situation. If you have been inaccurate in judgment or in placing responsibility, you are about to figure that out. You'll then be able to move forward with an open mind and honest action. The fundamental question you need to answer is one you are probably asked, in some context, every day.

What's Happening?

In our friendly American culture, we've all been conditioned to make such inquiries as: "What's up?" "How's it going?" "What's going on?" or "How's life?" And we've all been conditioned through their sheer repetition to ignore these questions or, at the very least, to dismiss them as unimportant.

"Everything is just fine." When we declare it so, you see, we can get right back on with the business of life—the high-energy, rapid-pace, emotionally charged anxiety of endless activity and unfinished stuff. And who can blame us? I mean, who wants to take the time to explain to every polite enquirer the reality of the events, circumstances, and complexities we are presently trying to handle?

Not me. I've often said that there are two types of busy people. Those who believe they are very busy and, when asked how they are doing, will tell you all about it in great detail for as long as it takes. That way they don't have to actually do any of it. Then there are those who are so busy they can't afford to take the time to tell you about it. They smile and acknowledge you, and they keep conversations brief and focused because they have lots to do.

But the question "What's happening?" takes on greater importance and depth when you ask it of yourself. And when you dare to answer that question with complete honesty, you undertake the next step in the process of living off balance on purpose. You "own" your reality.

Before you can make purposeful steps forward, you must know where you are starting from. It's not about looking forward and envisioning your dreams. Not yet. First you need to see your life as it is. Not better than it is (deceiving yourself by ignoring reality). Not worse than it is (bathing in the indulgence of victimhood). As it is. Now. This very moment.

Remember that the OBOP process has both macro and micro applications. It is certainly important to evaluate your life situation and take ownership of your reality in a big picture sort of way. That's the macro context. But where the rubber meets the road of life is in the day-to-day encounters—the conversations, tasks, decisions, and actions that take place moment to moment. That's the micro context. Some of these scenes are expected, planned for, and perhaps even rehearsed. Others are completely improvised.

Owning our realities is the way we find our footing, confidence, and basis for action. The problem is, far too often we rush headfirst into an encounter without taking a moment to pause and evaluate the reality.

What's happening? What's *really* happening? Give this vital question attention as you move through your day. Before responding to situations, inserting your efforts (or opinions) and doing something, pause to consider and observe the scene. It may take just a moment, or it may require some more careful study, but what you learn may truly surprise you. Over time, and with regular practice, this will become more natural and effortless—part of your routine. Before action, you'll take half a moment, a minute, or a month—whatever is required to accurately assess the reality of the circumstances—before forming an opinion, conclusion, or plan of action.

I'm not saying that if you have a ball in your hand, you should hold on to it or try to control situations by the very act of inactivity or indecision. But by "getting real," relative to both the outside forces at work (real-life circumstances) and the inside forces (your ability to act), you'll move through life with a greater sense of purpose and interest, and others will respond to you accordingly. And the actions you do take will be deliberate, positive, and aligned with your purpose.

Reality Check

When you are feeling overwhelmed or ungrounded, or if you are unsure of what you should do, it's always a good idea to conduct a quick "reality check" by mentally reviewing three fundamental truths:

1. You are here because of your past choices and actions.
2. The past is over.
3. You control what happens next.

Let's examine each of those powerful statements to get a full grasp on how to conduct this reality check.

REALITY ONE: YOU ARE HERE BECAUSE OF YOUR PAST CHOICES AND ACTIONS

Whatever you are presently experiencing is a direct result of your decisions. You can take full credit for your successes and missteps. Own your past. It's yours—bought and paid for with your time, money, and energy. Whatever pattern exists in your life right now, you created it.

Period.

This first point is often a deal breaker, an insurmountable hurdle for those who are unwilling to surrender their status of "aggrieved victim." It is difficult and humbling to claim credit for our shortcomings. Yet this step is truly the keystone requirement for making positive strides toward a more promising future.

Pride must take a backseat to progress. Pride and blame are soothing antiseptics, and when applied they can bring instant relief to life's pains. But upon closer examination, they merely mask the infections and cause greater inflammation and suffering. In contrast, humility is a true healing agent. When applied deliberately and consistently, it promotes the comfort that comes from within. Recovery always begins with a proper diagnosis.

"But what about life's unexpected tragedies? Illnesses? Crimes?" Granted, certain life events come at us with little explanation or warning. Please understand I am not assigning you personal blame for the tragic and inexplicable losses you will certainly face, nor for the actions of criminals against or upon you. There are times when we will be devastated by life events and will need to take time to absorb a loss or a disaster before moving on. Thankfully, most of our daily hardships are not of this sort. The majority of life's events are self-created circumstances that, left unchecked, take on unhealthy, powerful proportions, dominate our thinking, and forestall progress.

Even when events occur that are unexpected or out of our control, we can take responsibility for our *response* to those actions. "Aren't there times when I can feel justifiably victimized?" you might ask. Sure, you could feel that way if you want. But why bother? What good would it serve? What is the point? Feel free to blame whatever or whomever you like. Just realize that as long as this is your focus—however long you choose to assign responsibility to people and events outside your control—is exactly how long you forestall a solution. Why not skip all of that and claim responsibility for your actions within the situation? Focus on positive, deliberate action, not blame. This strategy will save you a great deal of time and energy.

REALITY TWO: THE PAST IS OVER

You can only begin from where you are now. The past is over. Let it go.

When you take ownership of your part in creating your life circum-stances—the good and the bad—then you must reconcile your culpability. Becoming honest and clear can be a liberating experience, but it also has some negative side effects. One of these is feeling guilty for misdeeds and wasted opportunities. When we take credit for our mistakes, it can be a humbling proposition.

Bemoaning the past, however, is simply another form of victimhood. Feeling bad about the events and encounters of old is a futile effort. It is a self-punishing exercise that forestalls positive action. You are, essentially, victimizing yourself.

When our words and deeds create problems for others, we create a trail of wreckage that must be dealt with eventually. Better to address these issues sooner rather than later. Take responsibility and apologize to those you may have wronged. Try to resolve issues, or at least express a willing-ness to admit your mistakes and ask for forgiveness. Then, forgive yourself and move on.

Interestingly, we can get similarly "stuck" by dwelling on past success. Perhaps the newsreel of your past is sensational. When you think back upon remarkable, enjoyable, wonderful moments and realize that you own that reality—you created it and can claim the credit—that feels pretty good. Reliving the "glory days" can provide an intoxicating escape from present circumstances. But if you are spending a significant chunk of your present moments pondering the past—whether you are reminiscing or ruminating—you are out of touch with your current reality. The past is over. Let it go.

Do not allow yourself to be handcuffed by history. Remove the shackles of regret and the chains of triumph. They are holding you back—restricting your expansion toward your infinite potential. Your greatest days are ahead of you. While it is important to learn from past experiences, recognize that the power of transformation is a present-day commodity, and it is, at this moment, within your grasp.

REALITY THREE: YOU CONTROL WHAT HAPPENS NEXT

The future will not be the same as the present; life is in a constant state of flowing change. While some circumstances may be unexpected, you control your response to these events, and therefore you can have a positive effect on the overall outcome.

Your success, happiness, and enjoyment of life depend upon no one but you. If you find yourself waiting for someone else to make a decision that will determine your happiness, you are in a vulnerable position indeed.

Certainly, you need others to help craft your reality, and the people in your life are significant influencers. Others contribute to your life experience or, in some cases, detract from it. But there is a big difference between an influencer and a determiner. You are the determiner. You are the final authority on your life. Do not relinquish that role to anyone else.

There is always something you can do to take a positive step forward. And the first step is a self-examination and a visit to the "Principles' Office."

Principles, Beliefs, and Values

I grew up in Chicago, a city full of character, culture, and phenomenal architecture. The skyline's centerpiece and iconic symbol of strength is, of course, the Sears Tower, which for twenty-eight years was the world's tallest building, standing at a proud 1,730 feet including the antennas. In September 2007, Sears was surpassed by Burj Dubai, a project that continues to climb even as I write this. Presently, Burj Dubai stands at 2,064 feet and is still under construction, with its maximum height a closely guarded secret (to thwart other designers and builders who are seeking the "world's tallest" title).

When you build something that big, it turns out to be extraordinarily heavy (Sears weighs more than 440 million pounds). To hold the structure in place and secure it against wind and weather, it must have one solid foundation. For Sears, this involved digging 70 feet to reach the solid bedrock before construction began. For Burj Dubai, 192 piles (reinforced concrete columns) are buried more than 164 feet into the sand. With every construction project, whether it is building a home or a soaring tower, the first task is always the same. Build the foundation. Without a formidable foundation to anchor the building to the earth, all other construction efforts would be uncertain and temporary.

As you think about constructing your future, you will want to build upon a foundation that will be stable and support growth and lasting changes. To accomplish this, you will need to go deep and anchor your beliefs, values, and principles. Take ownership of what they are and enhance them to support a soaring tower of potential. They are a part of your current reality, whether you have defined or acknowledged them or not, so you had better take the time to understand them before attempting to define your purpose.

What you believe and what you value most translate into your beliefs and values. These work hand in hand to create principles, or rules for life, which guide your behavior. We all have principles, even though they probably are not catalogued in any "official" way and even though you may not have given much thought to what they are. Think of beliefs, values, and principles as a structural system in which each element supports the next one. For example:

1. If you believe that most people are inherently good.

2. Then you will likely value people, relationships, diversity, and opportunities to learn from others.

3. These values will probably lead to such principles as:

   • Stay open to people and to multiple approaches to a situation. There's more than one right answer.

   • Nurture new relationships and maintain the ones you have.

   • Communication is essential.

But what if you had a different core belief? For example:

1. If you believe that most people are inherently corrupt, selfish, and dishonest.

2. Then you will likely value security, separation, protection of what you have and think, and a select group of people who think like you do—people you *can* trust.

3. These values will probably lead to such principles as:

   - Keep people at a distance.
   - Be skeptical of other people's motives; they are out to get something.
   - Security is essential; protect and defend ideas and property at all costs.

Do you think that these two differing sets of beliefs, values, and principles will result in you having different life experiences? I juxtaposed these two examples to point out that what you believe creates a chain reaction with your values and principles. What is most interesting and illustrative is that, in each case, the person has created a system of thought (beliefs and values) and action (guiding principles) that will confirm and perpetuate the beliefs he or she cherishes. The two individuals will both be proved right each and every day.

There is more than one reality. Our beliefs, values, and principles define and facilitate the reality we wish to experience. Above all else, we want to be proved right. So let's get real. What do you believe?

WHICH BELIEFS DO YOU HOLD?

"Love is hard to find."	or	"Love is all around us."
"I'm always broke."	or	"I am meant to be prosperous."
"There is never enough time."	or	"Every moment has infinite potential."
"I'll never be able to live my dream."	or	"Anything is possible."
"The world is falling apart."	or	"I can make a difference—small actions have a huge impact."
"Opportunity is limited."	or	"Opportunity is limitless."
"Staying in shape has always been a battle."	or	"I deserve to be healthy and fit."

"Quitting smoking is incredibly hard."	*or*	"I am capable of shedding old habits."
"I can't seem to find any life balance."	*or*	"Off balance is okay, as long as it's purposeful."
"I'm just not good enough."	*or*	"I'm doing my best and getting better."
"My spirit is always hurting."	*or*	"My spirit is healing and evolving."
"If I only had that, I'd be satisfied."	*or*	"I'm satisfied and content right now, right here."

Which "reality" would you rather have? That of the person on the left, who is broke, alone, in poor health, hurting, and hopeless? Or that of the person on the right, who is attracting love, health, prosperity, positive change, new opportunities, and greater potential? It's an easy call.

What do you believe? Are your beliefs beneficial to your long-term success and happiness, or do they need to be reshaped? You can change beliefs, and it's easier than you might think. Start by *suspending your disbelief*.

SUSPEND YOUR DISBELIEF

When you go see a movie, you sit down in a dark theater and watch, wide-eyed, as a series of implausible events and scenarios occur. When you surrender to the screen, anything is possible, from the incredible to the supernatural. And although we know that what we are watching is imagined, we "suspend our disbelief" temporarily so we can simply enjoy the ride.

I believe this is the same way you reshape a belief from limiting to empowering. Suspend your disbelief that your previous mental construct is the only right answer. Introduce the question: What if it was different?

For example, let's say you have a belief that maintaining your health is a constant struggle. You believe being healthy takes a supreme effort and requires difficult sacrifices. Deep down you know your life would be better if you did get in shape. But it's just too hard.

Like most beliefs, that is a persuasive statement, and it has been confirmed through your experience, so it is hard to simply flip a switch and suddenly believe something different. So, instead, just consider a possibility. What if it were possible that you could become healthier and maintain that condition without a monumental struggle? What if you could actually enjoy the process, and it was fun?

I'm not asking you to substitute a belief that is 180 degrees from your previous position. Doing battle with your beliefs is a losing proposition, because you'll likely become defensive, set yourself up for failure, and reconfirm your limitations. Instead, I'm just asking you to introduce the *possibility* that your beliefs could be different—more empowering—even temporarily. Just try the new belief on for size. Slip behind the wheel of a new belief system and take it for a test-drive; see if you notice a difference in performance. What would you value? What new principles would guide your life and inform your decisions? Enter the theater of your mind, where anything is possible, and suspend your disbelief that you are limited by the past. Imagine that you can have an amazing, fulfilling, blessed, healthful, and enjoyable existence. Then watch the story unfold.

Take Your Temperature

In the late 1970s, many fads swept the nation—disco, pet rocks, and Farrah Fawcett hair to name a few. I also recall the wild popularity of mood rings. These trendy and fashionable collectables were a huge hit because they allowed people to judge the mood of the wearer by observing the color of the stone in the ring. If you were mellow, relaxed, and friendly, the stone would appear a light green or blue, signaling that you were approachable. If, however, you were angry, excited, or anxious, the stone turned black.

Mood rings were a fun fashion statement and conversation piece. And for a time, some people believed that they were accurate. In fact, the rings worked on one simple principle—temperature. The "stone" is actually a glass capsule containing thermo-chromatic liquid crystal (or a clear quartz crystal with a layer of liquid crystal underneath it). This material shifts its color spectrum based on subtle changes in the body's temperature. Heat it up (by raising your internal temperature through activity or emotion or by standing in the sun, for that matter) and voilà! You've changed your mood.

With or without the accompanying jewelry, temperature has long been used as a way to characterize mood and temperament. Whether it corresponds to an accurate thermometer reading or not, we understand that some people are naturally cooler than others, and some can get hot with little or no provocation. How about you? Do you have a cool head or a heated temper? Are you all fired up, looking for conflict? Or are you able to chill, even in the midst of unexpected situations? What's your temperature?

As you continue to take ownership of your reality, take an honest look at your internal temperature. Answer these questions.

TAKE YOUR TEMPERATURE

- Are you happy, cheerful, and positive, or depressed, defeated, and usually negative?
- Is your sense of humor good-natured or sarcastic?
- Are you loving or skeptical?
- Are you able to stay calm when others become frantic, or do you add fuel to the fire?
- Do you create stress for yourself and for others, or are you capable of diffusing stress through calm thought and deliberate action?
- Do other people benefit from being around you, or do they view you as a challenge to tolerate?

Own up to your dominant mode of operation, that is, your emotional temperature, whatever it is. Then decide if it's acceptable to you or if it's something you can improve.

Know Your Limits, but Know You're Limitless

I've made a case that you will never reach your full potential because it is infinite. But that doesn't mean that you can do anything at all. We are all imbued with strengths and talents, and in other areas we are less capable. Nevertheless, I believe that by following your strengths and purpose, you will never run out of ways to improve, grow, and become better—whether it is a higher level of understanding or a spiritual evolution or a level of mastery with a specific skill that continues to become more refined with time and attention.

People who are excellent at what they do and immerse themselves in their greatest areas of interest and natural abilities are constantly discovering what they don't yet know. They continue to learn; the awakenings may be subtle, but they are profound. Are you doing what you love? Are you doing what you are great at? Let's take a quick inventory (and ownership) of your abilities. Answer these questions.

MINE YOUR RESOURCES

- What are your greatest strengths?
- What are you excellent at doing—your highest abilities?
- What are you most interested in learning?
- What are your best character traits?
- In what ways do others seek your input and assistance?
- When you were a child, what did you do for fun? What were the subjects of your daydreams and fantasies?
- If you could start all over and do something else with your life, what would you do?

Looking at your answers to these questions, honestly assess whether the life you have now is making maximum use of your natural abilities and talents. Are you doing what you love?

If you find that your life is congruent with your strengths, abilities, and interests, fantastic! If not, then you've just identified some of your greatest resources and incredible opportunities. That's awesome too! As we move forward with this process in the coming chapters, you'll be able to leverage these strengths to affect meaningful change for yourself and the people whose lives you touch.

But understanding and leveraging your strengths is just one side of the coin. Many of life's frustrations arise when we are operating from our weaknesses instead of our strengths. You might be a creative, big picture person who is brilliant at design and concept, but your abilities break down when it comes to number crunching and the management of details. Or perhaps you are a person with a head for numbers, statistical analysis, and bottom line management, yet you are challenged by projects that require creative expression.

As important as it is to know your strengths, it is equally essential to know where your skills and interests most often deteriorate. Own your reality, relative to these questions. Then you can make an honest assessment of which areas can be addressed and improved upon and which can be avoided or delegated to another person—one who is strong in the ways you are not.

KNOW YOUR LIMITS

- What are your weaknesses?
- What tasks or ideas cause you to lose interest and "tune out"?
- What are you fearful of undertaking?
- In what ways are you most vulnerable?
- What patterns of behavior make you feel disappointed with yourself?
- When you receive criticism, what is being criticized?
- How do you take constructive criticism?
- What's holding you back?

Time for Action

Understanding the concepts we've been discussing in this chapter is not enough. In the following pages, I'll describe concrete steps you can and should take if you are serious about this process of ongoing improvement. First things first, though: If you haven't done so yet, get a journal or start a file that serves as your special place to capture the valuable insights you will take from these exercises. Do these exercises before reading the next chapter so that you will be ready to take the second step toward an off balance on purpose life of fulfillment.

EXERCISE ONE—WHEN IN DOUBT, ZOOM OUT

This mental warm-up is so simple that you do it with your eyes closed! Find a quiet space and read through the instructions completely before performing this exercise. I first learned to do this when I began performing. The prospect of taking the stage was frightful to me and caused a lot of anxiety. But I learned that the emotions I was feeling at the time—stress and fear—could actually be converted to more positive and useful feelings—excitement and playfulness.

Take a moment right now to imagine yourself where you sit reading this lesson. Now, take an "outside view" of the situation. Instead of seeing through your own eyes, position your mind's eye above you, looking down at you in the chair. Then "zoom out" so that you are at the highest point in the room, on the ceiling, watching yourself. Got it? Good. Now, zoom out farther still, right through the ceiling and into the sky. Look down at the office building or home in which you are sitting and reading. Then continue outward in your mental image, past the clouds, through the layers of atmosphere and into space itself. From this vantage point, watch the earth below you, rotating around its axis in the star-filled galaxy.

In less than a minute, you have just created some personal objectivity. You most likely have a more detached (and less emotional) perspective of your life situation. If you didn't quite get there, do it again. The more you repeat this visualization technique, the more natural and effective it will become. So, return to this exercise anytime you need to get the big picture view.

EXERCISE TWO—DEAR SELF

Have you ever noticed how it's always easier to look at someone else's life and see their potential than it is to see your own? As an outside observer, we can clearly view their reality (or at least, we think we can). Positive choices become obvious because we are not emotionally attached to the outcomes. Maybe you've tried to share these insights with a friend. If so, you learned that a gentle, loving approach is extremely important. You are now about to take that approach with yourself, by writing a letter. I've even started it for you:

> *Dear Self (use your name),*
>
> *I've been thinking about you a lot lately, and I need to let you know what's on my mind. You see, I care about you very much and wanted to share a few observations about your life situation in the hopes that it may help you discover a fresh perspective. Please receive these comments in the loving spirit they are intended. The way I see it . . .*

This may be the most important letter you will ever write. Give it your serious commitment.

Own your reality. Don't rent it, lease it, borrow it, or lend it. Own it. It's not a time-share either, so make sure it's your reality, not someone else's reality of your life. It's personal. It's vital. It's ever changing. This moment's reality is different from when you started reading. You are different.

Starting right now, take increasing ownership of your reality. Give it thoughtful and careful attention. "What's happening," here, you see, is the beginning of your expansion toward greater fulfillment.

11

SEEK YOUR PURPOSE

AS I WRITE this chapter, I'm asking myself a question. Most likely, it's the same question you have in mind as you begin to read this chapter.

What's the point?

After all, your life is busy and there are many other things you could be doing right now. Is this worth your time? Is it purposeful? Step two of the OBOP process is to seek your purpose.

Purpose. What is it? How do you know when you have found it? And how can you stay focused on it when you are being pulled in many directions? Purpose is, after all, what makes it possible to be off balance, yet peaceful and productive. Purpose is the catalyst that inspires others and ignites infinite possibilities. Finding your purpose comes down to asking two basic questions:

- What do you want?

- Why do you want it?

And raising those two questions prompts you to ask one more: Which comes first, the "What" or the "Why"?

I think we often get this one wrong. We first decide *what* we want and construct a list of desired outcomes, material possessions, monetary gain, excursions, commitments, and aspirations. Then we strike out in pursuit of our "wants" without foresight, without knowing *why* we are pursuing those goals. The pursuit becomes the "why." And after attaining the objectives we sought, we may find them less fulfilling than we imagined they would be.

I believe we are better served by asking the why question before the what. That answer will offer us a much clearer insight into our motivations. We can then strike out with the confidence that our reasoning is sound and our purpose is understood and compelling.

Purpose Comes from You and Through You

Deep down, we want to be synchronized with what we deem to be valuable, meaningful, and truthful. We hunger for it, and without it, life becomes a rambling, pointless endeavor.

So why don't we all have it? If purpose is so important and universally desired, why doesn't everyone just go out and get some? What separates us from following, or even knowing, the "main thing about the main thing?" And how the heck do we figure it out? I hope to help you discover the direction of your purpose and take a few confident steps toward it.

You see, the quest for purpose is a lifelong endeavor. We uncover the answer a layer at a time, sometimes on a "need to know" basis. Your present understanding of your purpose on Earth will not be the same ten years from now. But you can only begin where you are. Own your present reality. Start the search. Join the hunt. Open your eyes to the possibility that your life is a divine gift—for you and for the world. Unwrap it. Peel back a layer at a time.

Does purpose come from you or through you? I think both.

I believe that we are all given gifts. Some of these gifts we are born with, and they present themselves as unique talents, interests, and abilities. These are clues to your God-given purpose, that is, the very reason you are here and the work you are meant to be doing.

But we also choose a purpose every day. We plan our actions. We set our goals. We make conscious choices about how we are going to spend our time. Then we choose whether we are going to stick to the plan or pick a different route entirely.

When the purpose that comes from you is in alignment with the purpose that flows through you, your life takes on joy and significance that is otherwise impossible to experience.

Stand in the middle of the road and you will surely get run over. Attempt to be all things in equal parts and you become diluted and insignificant. You lose your identity as well as your authority. What you say and think loses meaning and credibility because you are operating from an inauthentic platform.

To own your authenticity and wield true power in this world, you must operate from the inside out. Choose: good over evil, pros before cons, responsibility rather than abandonment. Over time, we can talk about how those choices averaged out, but in this moment—now—where life actually happens, you must make a choice. Pick one. Do it with confidence, from the core of who you are.

That's not always easy at first, but it becomes effortless when you are aligned with your purpose, when it is coming from you and through you.

Finding the Why

Finding your purpose is a lifelong process, but you will routinely get glimpses and clues if you ask the simple question "Why?" Why do you get up in the morning? Why do you go to work? Why is it important that you make certain changes in your life?

It seems as though my children ask the question "Why?" a hundred times a day. "Why do I have to go to bed? Why can't I watch TV instead of going to school? Why do I have to take a bath again? I took one yesterday." Okay. Those are a few slightly exasperating examples. But you know, the habit of asking "Why?" in response to the world is not really an act of defiance—not always. More often, it is an expression of curiosity and wonder. "Why does the Moon change shape, Daddy? Why do some people have to live on the street? Daddy, why do you have to leave to go on a work trip again?" Those types of questions are genuine, heartfelt quests for meaning—for understanding—for purpose.

Cultivate (or perhaps I should say rediscover) the habit of asking why in some of the situations you've come to take for granted. When you encounter an especially challenging circumstance, asking "Why?" will help you clarify just how important it is. If it is unimportant, then maybe you'll reevaluate whether you should do it. But if you can crystallize and quantify the meaning behind it, and keep that in mind, you'll find the difficult challenges get easier, and the rewards become so much more satisfying.

Also ask "Why?" before you start a meeting, engage someone in conversation, or plan an important project. Asking that simple question forces you to frame your experiences in a context that is connected to purpose. That perspective will enable you to more easily identify your values, formulate life principles, and set meaningful goals. Each of these elements plays an important part in the purpose equation.

As Rick Warren wrote in the opening line of his best seller *The Purpose Driven Life*, "It's not about you." Your purpose is not self-serving. It's not about you. Your purpose is somehow related to serving others and providing care, comfort, and value. You will know you have found your purpose (or, at least, are getting darn close) when you find yourself becoming excited, frightened, focused, and validated by external forces. In that sense, falling into purpose is a lot like falling in love.

ACTIVE INTROSPECTION

Purpose doesn't announce itself at your doorstep, but it certainly leaves clues for you to follow. Often these clues reside in our feelings and responses to our world. When you get excited, angry, elated, or distraught, pay attention. Emotions like joy, excitement, and wonder are powerful triggers that alert us to the ideas and experiences that fulfill us. Conversely, when we feel anger and disgust when we see injustice, poverty, or plight, we are connecting to a passion we have to affect change in these areas. Trust your gut, and follow these clues to your purpose.

In your notebook, continue the work you began in the previous chapter when you started to mine your resources. But here, try to focus on the emotional, gut-level response you have to these questions. Answer them quickly—your first response is likely to be accurate. Be truthful and fearless. In this exercise you're just trying to uncover the clues. You aren't obligated to do anything with the answers. Just knowing will be a powerful step. You'll have improved insight and awareness relative to your purpose. As your perception improves, so will your self-discovery.

CLUES TO YOUR PURPOSE

- If you could change one thing about the world, what would it be?
- When do you feel most alive?
- If money were not an issue, what would you do? What would you learn?
- What are you truly excellent at doing?
- What endeavors and activities do you enjoy most? What causes you to lose track of time?
- What fascinated you as a child? What fascinates you now?
- What do you desire most? Why?
- In what way can you be of greatest service to others?
- If you knew you had five years to live, what would you do? How about six months?
- What is the best way you know to uplift and celebrate others?

Having given those questions careful thought and honest answers, you have just created a gold mine of clues to your purpose. This is the "stuff" you care about—the pursuits that truly matter to you. Reexamine your answers and see if you can find patterns or consistent themes that continue to come up. These are aspects of who you are and what you were created to accomplish. Don't discount those ideas another day. Embrace them!

It's not enough, however, simply to know what you care about. Bring these interests, passions, and skills into your daily experience. Are you sharing your gifts with others?

MAKE AN ALIGNMENT ADJUSTMENT

Identify one thing you can do to improve the alignment between your purpose and your daily actions. In other words, how can you design your life so that it reflects your uniqueness, your passions, and the joy you can share with others? The answer might be as big as a new career move or simply a subtle shift of focus. Get clear on your alignment adjustment—then DO IT!

Here's a very personal example based on the journal I kept during my month in the Middle East.

Sunrise in Afghanistan. On day six of the Armed Forces Entertainment Tour—the most purposeful event in my performance career—our Blackhawk helicopter raced over the terrain at more than 150 miles an hour and just one hundred feet above the ground, doors open. If the pilots were trying to give us a thrill to remember, it most certainly worked. We were heading to the forward operating base in Jalalabad.

As gratifying and humbling as events had been so far, the true lesson in the experience—the thing that changed me forever—was the example of the men and women we lived with, performed for, and witnessed in action. You could not help but be awed by their effort and commitment.

When the two Blackhawks landed in Jalalabad, we swirled up a cloud of dust as well as the interest of soldiers and Afghanis alike. The primary purpose for this team of soldiers, most of whom hailed from Iowa, was to reach out to the local community and build both infrastructure and relationships. A dozen or more Afghanis, some former fighters, were employed on the base to help with cooking meals, transporting materials, and other important tasks.

American soldiers venture into the local community every day to construct roads, schools, water systems, and other vital resources for the people who live there. Not all of their efforts are initially understood or appreciated (evidenced by the stack of unused school desks that are piled up in one of the buildings—no one wanted to use them). But over time progress was being made.

One story that was shared casually during our base tour conveys the essence of who these soldiers are at their core, and how they persist in such trying circumstances. Three months before our visit, at Christmastime, care packages had arrived from friends and family back home. You can imagine the joy they all experienced (they don't get much mail to begin with) to be connected to something so familiar and wonderful as holiday celebrations with loved ones.

Considering the piles of packages, cards, and letters, the idea took hold that this wasn't something to keep to themselves. So they loaded the bounty into a Humvee, drove into town, and gathered a crowd.

"These are from our families back in the United States," they told the citizens, using translators. "They sent them to us to celebrate the holiday, and we would like to share them with you." Then the soldiers opened each gift before an increasingly excited audience—and gave everything away.

"The gifts were an opportunity to extend our real mission and to build relationships. After all, that's why we are here."

"That's why we are here." What a beautiful example of living off balance on purpose. They weren't acting on orders. The soldiers at Jalalabad were so connected to the meaning of their mission that they were able to further the important work they were doing, but they also strengthened the lifelines between their relationships with family and friends back home and the mysterious, dangerous work they were doing half a world away. Do you think their families were disappointed after learning that their presents were "instantaneously regifted"? Not a chance. I'd be willing to wager they felt honored to help—to be a part of the purpose. I sure did.

The Purpose of the Moment

Seeking purpose, like the rest of the OBOP process, applies to both the big picture questions as well as your daily activities. Without purpose to your daily pursuits, you are simply playing Whac-A-Mole with tasks, bopping whichever ones pop up, without any sense of meaning. Before you start another item on your "to do" list, ask yourself, "Why am I doing this?" Answer the question completely and thoughtfully before you take action. It will take just a few moments, but you will notice a remarkable difference in your clarity and momentum.

Apply the same technique to conversations you have, both in person and over the telephone. Instead of just "winging it"—starting a dialogue to see where it goes—decide in advance what you want to contribute or get out of the time you spend with someone. Invest purpose into the relationship. The purpose might be a specific business objective, such as closing a sale, getting a recommendation, or providing input to help guide a decision. Or perhaps in a personal conversation, it could be to deepen a valuable relationship, to express an opinion in a way that it is heard and appreciated, or simply to listen with an open mind and loving heart.

Living "on purpose" is an intentional act and a daily commitment. With practice, it becomes a habit—an extension of who you are. Sure, you'll be challenged, tempted, distracted, and seduced to stray from your mission. That's why you need frequent (and emotionally charged) reminders.

PURPOSEFUL REMINDERS

Purposeful reminders are like road signs to keep you pointed in the right direction and to help ensure that you get to your desired destination. By building up a platoon of reinforcements, you'll find it far easier to seek your purpose in the flow of day-to-day living.

You already started setting up some purposeful reminders when you identified your beliefs, values, and principles in the previous chapter. And when you uncover the layers of the purpose inside you, you can take additional steps toward ensuring that your path is well lit and easier to follow. Remind yourself constantly with purpose-feedback mechanisms.

Get Visual
The best reminders engage us emotionally and stimulate strong feelings that connect us to the "why" of our workload. To get emotional, you need to get visual, using photos, quotes, lists, written goals—whatever most reminds you of what you want and why it is important.

Do you hope one day to send your child to a fantastic college and provide him or her with world-class educational opportunities? Put up a photo of your son or daughter alongside a photo of a happy college graduate or a prestigious university.

Do you find letters you've received from clients and customers telling you what a difference you've made in their lives gratifying? Don't stick them in a drawer. Put the letters in a prominent place where you will see them regularly.

Do you envision a positive change in your community, industry, or world? Are you working toward the solution? Decide what that will look like and then post it on your office, bedroom, or bathroom wall. (Bathroom mirrors are excellent places for reminders, because we see them at the beginning and the end of every day.)

The same is true for your favorite quotes, mantras, beliefs, and principles. Keep them in front of you where you can see them again and again.

Each day, you are bombarded by negative news stories, persuasive advertisements, and plentiful distractions that will all combine to sidetrack your thinking and focus. Combat those forces with a proactive visual support system that will help you see and pursue your purpose. The following story from my tour in the Middle East illustrates what I mean:

In Bagram, Afghanistan, in the base commander's office, hangs a large (3 foot by 4 foot) photo of a little girl. This Afghani child was no more than six years old, yet the expression on her face bore the hardship and experience of a lifetime. She sat on the barren ground and was looking at the camera with a sense of gratitude. Perhaps it was for the gift she had received and was presently using to stay warm. You see, she was wrapped tightly in an American flag. The commander told me that this powerful image symbolized an important aspect of their mission. They were in Afghanistan not only to rout those who would do harm to America but also to support and foster an oppressed and wounded population. He wanted to restore hope by "wrapping" the citizens, especially the children, in the comfort of American protection as well as the idea that they all deserved to be treated with dignity.

In your efforts to create emotionally engaging reminders, you might consider putting together a "Dream Board." Create a collage of photographs, drawings, quotes, and other visual reminders to help you envision the life you desire. Include a photo of someone with the physique you aspire to have, images of the trips you plan to take and the lifestyle you desire, and most important, photos that convey the positive impact you intend to have on others. Whatever that looks like—whether it's a photo that captures the smiling faces of the lives you will touch or a tangible project you will see through to completion—it is important to keep those aspirations fixed in your mind. A Dream Board or various well-placed visual reminders will help you do so.

Choose Your Team

Before any game or battle begins, you need to first choose sides. Start by asking yourself, "If I could choose anyone at all, who would I enlist to support me in my pursuits?" Decide who you want to be like, and learn as much as you can about them. When it comes to seeking our purpose, it isn't a solo pursuit. We all need mentors and role models to show us the way and help us crystallize our vision.

The great thing about role models is that you don't even need their permission! Choose anyone at all—famous or familiar, past or present, living or deceased—who embodies the qualities you deem most important and useful in your purposeful pursuit. Then get to know those people, in person, by reading about them, or by studying their works and writings. Draw these people close to you by thinking of them as like you. Ask yourself what they would do in your situation, and then model your behavior after theirs. But always be authentic to yourself.

Mentors take a more interactive role in our lives, and for this you do need permission. Enlist the help of someone more experienced and capable. Share your passion and purpose with mentors and ask intelligent, well-reasoned questions. If you demonstrate a willingness to take action and deliver the necessary effort to learn and grow, you will certainly be able to find a person who will share valuable experience, guidance, and encouragement with you. The key is that you earn the respect of your mentor by demonstrating your ability to accept suggestions and make changes. If you ask for help and then fail to implement what you learn, your mentor will likely withdraw his or her support and reduce the investment of time, emotion, and energy in your future.

I don't think life was meant to be inherently difficult, frustrating, or painful. We certainly can make it that way by insisting on choices that steer us from our purpose. Sadly, we can persist on this path to the point of self-destruction.

In every situation, no matter how challenging, there is a purpose to be discovered. Seek it! Ask the brave question that will aim your actions: why? The answer may change as you discover different aspects of your purpose throughout your lifetime. Fortunately, you don't have to have the entire answer before you get started on a purposeful path.

Next, we are going to lean forward and initiate exciting changes that will deliver results!

12

LEAN FORWARD AND MAKE YOURSELF UNCOMFORTABLE

RIDING A TALL unicycle teaches a person a great deal about balance as well as commitment. In fact, this illustration is so powerful I use it in nearly all of my presentations.

Often after the program, someone asks me, "So, how do you get that on the airplane?" The answer is, I don't. I actually have five unicycles, each measuring six feet in height (when assembled), packed in travel cases along with five sets of my other unusual (and hard-to-transport props), which include knives, battle axes, and bowling balls. We ship these cases in advance to the hotels or convention centers where I am scheduled to speak, playing a logistical game of leapfrog from one city to the next. It's worth all of the effort, though, because it helps me perfectly illustrate the third step in the OBOP process.

To make forward progress atop the six-foot unicycle, you must literally start falling toward your face. This is uncomfortable. The sensation of plunging into the great unknown with nothing to hold on to can be unnerving, to say the least. But only once you have thrown yourself off balance do you start pedaling—chasing your body with the unicycle so that you don't crash and suffer serious injury.

If you are hesitant to lean forward, that is, to try something new and uncomfortable, you will sail right off the back of the unicycle, ending your attempt before it even began. Or you might even start going backward. When you are riding in reverse, it becomes much more difficult to anticipate the next move and to steer around obstacles. Similarly, if we don't challenge ourselves and use our talents (lean forward), the skills we have developed will atrophy. If we don't continue to learn, we become less resourceful and relevant, and therefore also ineffective contributors to the world.

Sometimes in life, especially after we have achieved some measure of success, we become bent on simply maintaining what we have—whether it is status, skill, finances, or relationships. We just want to stay where we are because it is known and comfortable. We are successful, after all. We've arrived, and we just want to stay put, thank you. In unicycle terminology, this is called idling—pedaling forward and backward and forward and backward in order to stay in the same spot. You aren't falling off (which you would do if you stopped pedaling) but you aren't going anywhere either.

And yet many of us get into a rhythm of idling through life. We go forward a little bit, but when it gets uncomfortable, we go backward. Forward, then backward, to keep ourselves in check. Forward and backward, alternating between growth and stagnation, conquest and complacency, development and decay. As it is on a unicycle, there is no such thing as standing still in life. You are either moving forward or backward. Your choice. And the degree to which you accept control and initiate change in order to move forward is directly related to your growth potential.

If you truly desire forward progress in any area of life, you need to lean forward. Initiate action, even before you know how it's going to turn out. This prospect, I know, can trigger feelings of uncertainty, anxiety, or even fear. But let's call those feelings by a different name: excitement. It's normal and wonderful to feel excited about your life and the new possibilities that are coming your way. Embrace the excitement, lean forward, make yourself uncomfortable, and enjoy the thrill of the ride!

Make Yourself Uncomfortable

We understand how easy it is for others to make us uncomfortable or for situations to make us uncomfortable. But how can we actively employ this technique in our lives? There are endless examples, and you probably already have an idea of what you need to do next. Hint: It's the thing that makes you squirm a bit when you think about it. But I'll contribute some ideas to get the ball (or unicycle) rolling.

MAKE A COMMITMENT TO SOMEONE YOU RESPECT

We all need others in order to grow. We need the input of experienced people who have mapped the roads we endeavor to travel. We may need collaborators whose expertise provides a complementary match to our own skills and attributes. And often we simply need a sounding board, a receptive ear, a chance to broadcast our intentions to another person. This simple act of speaking our desires and plans instantly makes our imaginings more tangible.

> For years, I intended to write a book by the title *Success in Action*. I knew it was a necessary step for my career and my message, yet the challenge was so daunting, I did not know how to begin. Then a good friend and speaking colleague, Curt Boudreax, heard my intention and made me accountable. "I'm buying the first book, Dan. Now write it." Curt handed me a twenty-dollar bill as he said those words. I carried that bill in my day planner for months, and it made me increasingly uncomfortable. The twenty represented a commitment I made to a mentor (and a customer), and it was just the incentive I needed to lean forward and take action. When the first shipment of books arrived, Curt got the first one out of the box, along with a note of thanks and an invoice stamped "Paid in Full."

SCHEDULE A "LAUNCH DATE"

If you have been intending to make a positive change "one of these days," why not go ahead and pick one? Take a lesson from our space program.

NASA schedules months in advance the precise day, minute, and second of every rocket launch. The coordinated efforts of hundreds of intelligent experts are synchronized to a time line to meet the planned moment for liftoff. I recently had the chance to attend a Space Shuttle launch at Kennedy Space Center with my son and my father. I've always wanted to witness a launch with my own eyes and experience the awesome force (7 million pounds of thrust) that it takes to accelerate the shuttle from a standstill to five times the speed of sound in less than two minutes.

Space Shuttle orbiter *Discover*, flight STS-124, launched flawlessly on May 31, 2008. The scheduled (and actual) departure time was 5:02 p.m. and twelve seconds. If you have ever wondered why the timing is so exact, it has to do with the desired path of the flight. At that precise moment, the shuttle had its most direct route to the intended destination: in this case, a docking with the International Space Station (ISS). The "launch window" was a narrow ten minutes, after which the mission would have to be "slipped" to a later time and date, when the Earth and the orbit of the ISS were once again in alignment.

It's possible that the window for your "launch" isn't so narrow, but how will you know when the right time is if you don't assess the ideal circumstance for liftoff and create a plan to get you there? If you want to marshal the power of a "scheduled launch," determine when the conditions will be ideal for your assent into the stratosphere. Allow enough advance time for the necessary preparations, and then post the date and let the countdown begin.

GO TO CLASS

For some people, going to a class seems like a very safe, comfortable environment. For others, it is not so inviting. Regardless of where you are on this spectrum, seeking education can be a way to lean forward and get uncomfortable in a good way.

Whatever you wish to learn, do, or become, there is a class that can help you. But classes can be challenging. If you don't know a foreign language but have always wanted to learn one, you might be uncomfortable with the idea of trying to do so in front of other people. If you have been trying to finish a degree program but you haven't fulfilled a math require-ment because you think you might fail the required math class, enrolling in that class might make you uncomfortable.

You don't have to quit your day job and enroll in a university pro-gram. Test the waters with a weekly online course you can work into your schedule. Whatever your interest, from acting to zoology, you can find instruction. Where to look? Start with community colleges, adult continu-ing education programs, and specialized schools in your area of study (lan-guages, computers, cooking, etc.). It may surprise you, but many stores and corporations offer classes at very reasonable prices. For instance, Home Depot teaches classes in woodworking, tiling, plumbing, wallpapering, and more. Apple Inc. has a wide assortment of free or inexpensive Mac com-puter classes at their retail stores. PGA Tour Superstore will teach you a golf swing for $25 per lesson.

Why? Providing education to interested people and getting them to come to the store is how stores attract customers and make sales. Interested in a more specialized skill, such as unicycling, music, or mountaineering? You may need to seek out a private instructor or join a club. Sure, it may cost a little money, but the investment in your future will be well worth the price. And that leads us to the next strategy.

PUT YOUR MONEY WHERE YOUR MOUTH IS

An investment of time, thought, and energy certainly demonstrates your commitment. But for some people and certain situations, an investment of money is required to truly lean forward and initiate an empowering, off-balance posture. Talk is cheap; what we spend our money on, however, demonstrates what we truly value. So, invest in that class, the next phase of your business, or a commitment to improving your health. Step up your financial reflection of your faith by giving more money to your church or donating to a cause you believe in. Spend money, as well as time, to enhance the relationships you value.

In equal measure, limit or cease your spending on aspects of life that are contrary to your principles. When you do an accounting of your check-book, credit cards, and cash, where does it all go? The adage "You get what you pay for" is equally true in this sense. You are the person you demonstrate through the dollars you spend. If your checkbook is out of alignment, your life is likely out of alignment as well.

SELL IT FIRST, FIGURE IT OUT LATER

I've been in the entertainment business for most of my life. Over the years, I've received many unusual requests for shows. Some involved special themes and costumes (ten-foot-tall, stilt-walking aliens, for example). Others required specific stunts and skills (like juggling fire torches standing inside a steel globe while motorcycles raced around my body). Sometimes the client wanted me to assemble a full-scale production involving a dozen circus performers, customized music, lighting, and staging (no problem). Of course, I didn't say yes to every request—some were not suited to my skill set or interests. Other times the client or venue was questionable—out of alignment with my principles or character.

By selecting ones that did suit me, I built a business by being able to deliver what I promised. And many, many times I promised (and sold) something I had never done before.

I paid for my college education by performing comedy variety shows and producing entertainment. I was in my freshman year when a call came in from a prospective client who wanted me to juggle fire at a "Polynesian Party." No problem, I told her; I had been juggling fire for years and could put on a sensational show for them.

When the client called back a day later and modified her request, she explained that her requirement was not for "fire juggling" but "fire eating." This was an important distinction. I had never "eaten" fire in my life. I had seen my mentor eat fire, but because I was only twelve years old when he and I started working together, my mother told me fire eating was off-limits. And I had never gotten around to learning since then.

But now I was in college. I was in business for myself. I was hungry. "Sure, I can do that. I can eat fire at your party as well as juggle it. No problem."

I hung up the phone and called my mentor, imploring him to teach me to eat fire . . . over the phone! He was understandably reluctant. But when I explained that I had already sold the show and there was no turning back, he agreed to help me. After all, the show must go on. So, with the help of a semi-willing mentor, a video camera to monitor my progress, and the commitment of having already sold this performance, I successfully learned to eat fire. Not only did I gain another booking, I made a new addition to my repertoire (and a great "party trick" for college) as well. Sometimes, in order to lean forward and initiate change, you have to sell it first and figure it out later.

A note of caution: If you do this too much in your day-to-day life, you will never be able to meet the commitments you make. After all, there is only so much time available each day for the "figure it out" part. And you have to be sure that you have the time and a path for figuring it out. If not, you're just making empty promises.

DEVELOP YOUR SPONTANEOUS SIDE

A well-reasoned, rational argument is required for certain situations. If, for example, you are an attorney about to deliver the closing statement for a complex case to an unconvinced jury, you probably shouldn't "wing it." When making a major purchase, like a house, car, or investment, it is usually a good idea to slow down the process, unearth all of the facts, list the pros and cons, and then distill a thoughtful decision. But sometimes, you need to trust your gut, welcome an unexpected encounter, and celebrate spontaneity.

"Spontaneous" is a good thing. Check the dictionary; spontaneous means "done or produced freely; naturally occurring." In other words, when you are in tune with your environment, when you are comfortable with who you are and what you want, events and circumstances will "naturally" present themselves to you. Learn to "go with the flow," embrace those opportunities when they come, and be a part of the active and organic process that unfolds.

If you are a person who has to have all of the facts and details in advance, cultivating your spontaneous side will be a worthwhile challenge. Start small by "scheduling spontaneity." Pick an afternoon to spend by yourself. Plan nothing but the date and time. When the moment arrives (and not a minute before), flip open a local newspaper or jump on the Internet and search for events in your area. Then decide. Make a choice and do what feels right, fun, and interesting. Then see what happens. If you're inclined to "plan spontaneity," resist the temptation to develop specific options in advance. To the best of your ability, keep it open-ended until the moment of decision.

This is a safe (and fun) way to push yourself into a new, unfamiliar realm. And it is really best to do this (at least initially) as a solo exercise. When you involve another person, you are placed in the position of balancing your decision with someone else's. It becomes a negotiation: "What do you want to do?" "I don't know. What do you want to do?"

LEARN TO IMPROVISE

For a crash course in spontaneity, enroll in an improvisation class. You can usually find an improv workshop or course at a local theater school, acting workshop, or comedy club. You don't have to be a performer to try it. You don't even have to be naturally funny. What you will learn will be a series of games, or scenarios, in which you will interact with other people in real time.

What comes out of this interaction might be funny. It often isn't. The goal is not to "go for the joke" but to live in the moment, be truthful to the situation, and focus intently on the other person. You will literally learn to "act before you think," and you'll find yourself saying and doing things without any expectations or forethought. If that sounds a bit scary . . . well, it is. But it can also be a liberating, character-expanding exercise. After all, you will be learning these techniques in a safe environment, free from criticism or expectations. And along the way you'll learn wonderful lessons for leaning forward and embracing uncertainty, such as the following:

Trust Your Instincts
Improv happens so fast that you don't have time to reason out options. Your partner needs a response from you immediately, and you are expected to deliver it. Once you learn to bypass your "filter," you'll experience a freedom of expression and interaction that is truly exhilarating. Avoid putting

pressure on yourself to think of something clever. Relax, have fun, and let your instincts take charge.

Make Bold Choices

When placed in a "scene," you are often given ridiculous characters or contrived circumstances that would never inhabit reality. The freedom to validate those choices and contribute your own can be exciting, fun, and liberating. A general rule is not to go for the first thought or "obvious" choice. Instead, think one or two steps beyond the obvious and take your second- or third-generation idea. All of this happens in the blink of an eye, but when you go with a bold choice and present it confidently, you'll see that new possibilities (and sometimes very funny moments) spontaneously materialize.

Just Say "Yes"

The cardinal rule of improvisation is to avoid the most destructive word to the forces of creativity. That word is "no." The moment you say "no" in response to an idea or suggestion from your improv partner, you bring the wheels of wonder to a grinding halt. Perhaps as the scene was developing, you had a great idea about where you wanted it to go—a sensational joke or scenario you wanted to insert later. Yet something your partner added took a detour that would not accommodate your brilliant notion. In an effort to "steer" the scene, you might say "not that way!"

The instant you say "no, but" you've stopped the scene cold and killed the chemistry among you, your partner, and the audience. Improv teaches you to abandon long-term plans and live in the moment. No matter how unexpected or off base the line or suggestion presented to you, accept it. Go with it. Say "yes, and" instead of "no, but." When you say "yes, and," you not only affirm the idea presented to you but also advance it by contributing your own suggestions.

This is a great rule for life. It takes guts to present an idea, whether you are on stage or off. In order to get to the best solutions and build the strongest partnerships, resist the temptation to point out the flaws you see or problems you anticipate. Start by validating what you like. Say yes to what you agree with. Then contribute your own suggestions to advance the idea in a desirable direction.

Making the Rounds

By cultivating an openness to the unplanned you become willing to lean forward and make yourself uncomfortable. This changes your life posture and unlocks possibilities that never before existed. You will quickly become more adaptable and more capable, and unexpected detours might just turn out to be far more fulfilling than the initial plans.

We were stuck in Bagram, Afghanistan. Our convoy into Kabul was cancelled because the personnel and equipment that would transport us to our performance was needed elsewhere. But the base commander requested that we make use of the downtime by visiting the base hospital to lift some spirits. We were, of course, happy to oblige.

When we arrived at the hospital, I expected to see American troops who were injured or ill. That was not the case. True, the medical staff and doctors were all U.S. military personnel, but the patients were all Afghani locals. They were victims of land mine explosions, gunshots, and other misfortunes.

In the hospital, there were no rooms to separate patients, just thin curtains between beds, hardly enough to shield one from the graphic realities of this war-torn country. Patients ranged in age from three to ninety. They spoke no English, and they were all around us, several missing legs, others badly scarred, burned, or in pain from less obvious injuries.

Without a doubt, we were out of place. We were uncomfortable. We didn't know what to do, and for a moment I thought the best course would be retreat. We were certainly off balance, but after glancing around at one another, we remembered that there was a purpose to our presence, and we were expected to follow through.

I approached a three-year-old girl named Cabannah, who was in a wheelchair, her limbs and head bandaged and her face revealing the burns that covered most of her body. She had been walking with her grandpa, who was carrying a container of gasoline—a leaky bag that caught a spark from a nearby stove and erupted in flames. They had both been badly burned.

I began to think of my own little Maggie, and I reached into my jacket pocket and removed a crystal ball. I rolled it along my hands and body, creating the illusion that it was floating in midair. I added another sphere, than another, working up to five at once. I broke my concentration to look at Cabannah. Something miraculous happened—she smiled. Her family members, gathered around her, also smiled and nodded, which gave me all of the encouragement I needed to continue.

Meanwhile, my friend Todd spun a ball on his finger for an eleven-year-old girl. He held out his hand and gestured for her to take the ball on her finger. From her wheelchair she reached forward and transferred the ball from his finger to hers. As I watched, I noticed that both her arms and legs were bandaged and that she had scars on her face from a buried Russian land mine that had riddled her with shrapnel. We only learned later that she had been unwilling to use her arm until this moment, refusing to even allow the doctors to take her blood pressure. The doctors were not even sure she could move it until, just then, caught up in the spirit of play, she became willing to show us all.

Encouraged by our audience's reaction, we started to throw juggling clubs to one another, passing them around the doctors, patients, and family members. We did acrobatics in the narrow space between beds. Everyone was engaged and uplifted, laughing and cheering us on! What started as a very uncomfortable moment was now a gigantic emotional release, and it felt fantastic.

We spent about an hour performing at the hospital, and every person in the place smiled that day. I know we gave them only a temporary interruption to their pain and difficulty. But I like to think that they remember us and smile occasionally. Who knows? One thing is for sure, however. We will never be the same again. What began as an uncomfortable excursion ended up being an immensely rewarding and life-changing event.

The Ratio of Risk and Reward

If the thought of implementing the suggestions I've made makes you a little uncomfortable . . . well, that's the point! Comfort and complacency rarely give rise to greatness. With these ideas, I am trying to give you some specific action items to stimulate your own thinking. I believe that any of these ideas, if implemented, will get you started and improve your tolerance for "leaning forward." But perhaps the best approach for you will be something else, a spontaneous opportunity that is born from your present circumstances, your heartfelt desires, and your perception of what is just a bit "risky."

Risk is relative, and it is entirely a matter of perception. One person would think nothing of free-climbing a 100-foot cliff, while another is fearful of leaving his own home. Most of us are somewhere in between. The key to this step in the OBOP process is to become aware of your own attitudes toward risk and to be willing to turn aversion into acceptance for a meaningful reason. When you have a meaningful reason to lean forward—when you are aligned with a persuasive purpose—discomfort transforms into excitement.

Here's a quick risk assessment that will help you get past emotional reflexes and shift your perception. Answer these questions, relative to the choice or circumstance you are contemplating.

- What is the immediate best thing that can happen?
- What are the long-term rewards?
- What is the worst thing that can happen?
- Is the worst thing acceptable? Can I live with it?
- What is the likelihood that the worst thing will happen?
- What forms of preparation and precautions can lessen the likelihood of the worst-case scenario? How effective will they be?
- Is the reward worth the risk?

RISK ASSESSMENT FORMULA

Think of this as a mathematical Risk Assessment formula:

$$BT + R \neq (WT - A) \times (L - P)$$

BT = *Best Thing*. On a scale from 1 to 50, with 1 representing a small positive outcome and 50 representing a "dream come true" scenario, how would you characterize the immediate impact of your best-case scenario?

R = *Ongoing Rewards*. We're going to use this number to beef up the "best case" side of the equation. This represents the ongoing benefits you will gain into the foreseeable future. They could be tangible, monetary, and concrete. Or, perhaps the rewards are less tangible but equally significant, such as a boost to self-confidence or self-esteem. In a business case, this could also represent your market position or future potential business. Again, pick a number from 1 (very minimal long-term impact) to 50 (maximum long-range benefit).

WT = *Worst Thing*. This time, use a scale from 1 to 100. The number 1 indicates a non-issue and 100 means "total devastation."

A = *Acceptability*. This will be an adjustment to the "worst case" side of the equation. Use a scale from 1 to 50, but with the higher number being positive: 1 means that this is not acceptable at all (it would be really hard to recover from a negative outcome) and 50 indicates that you could recover from this without much difficulty, even though it would initially have a negative impact.

L = *Likelihood*. This is represented as a percentage (or as a decimal) that the worst thing will happen (.10 means that there's a 10 percent chance of it happening). Be as honest and objective as possible.

P = *Precautions and Preparation*. This is an adjustment to the likelihood percentage. If you were totally prepared and took the necessary precautions, by what percentage would that lower the likelihood of a negative outcome?

Notice that this equation does not have an equal sign between the two sides. It has a "does not equal" sign, because the chances of the reward and the risk being equal are miniscule at best. Instead, one side will always be greater than the other. The results will vary, of course, depending on the unique circumstances you face.

When the reward side is greater than the risk side, the best thing that could happen plus the potential long-term rewards are greater than the worst-case possibilities. Perhaps this is because the worst thing that could happen really isn't that bad, or the likelihood of it happening is extremely low. Here, the situation really isn't as risky as you may have first perceived it to be. Go for it!

Here are some real-world examples to help you understand how to use the risk assessment formula.

Reward Greater than Risk Examples

If the worst thing that can happen is substantial, and maybe even likely, you still may find there are things you can do to minimize the risk. You can take precautions and prepare well for possible risks. And the potential reward is enormous—the fulfillment of a lifelong dream, for example. In this situation, you might find that the best thing and the rewards associated with it are still worth the risk.

First example—Getting on an airplane to travel across the country. The worst thing, in this case an airplane crash, would be horrendous. Yet the likelihood of it happening is extraordinarily small. Thus, the reward of being able to quickly get where you are going outweighs the adjusted risk.

Second example—Investing a significant amount of money and time in order to start a business. You could easily lose it all, which would have a huge initial negative impact. But in time, you could recover. The potential rewards of doing what you love and gaining enormous satisfaction and experience may make it a worthwhile and admirable endeavor. Again, acceptable risk is subjective, as is the magnitude of the successful outcome.

Risk Greater than Reward Examples

If the worst thing that can happen is devastating and intolerable, and it is a likely outcome, then that side of the equation will be greater than the reward side, and you should avoid the risk. It's simply not worth it.

First example—Engaging in questionable activity (such as a shady business deal or creative accounting) for a potential profit or enhanced level of status or success. Even if the chance of being found out (the risk) is relatively low, the potential devastation would ruin your career and your reputation. Also, the fact that the potential reward would come at the cost of your principles would greatly diminish its worth. This isn't an appropriate way to "make yourself uncomfortable."

Second example—Riding your bicycle off the garage roof in order to make an audition tape for the next "Jackass" movie. (Any action that starts with the words "Hey, watch this!" probably falls into this category.)

If you were to run the numbers of such a stunt, it might look like this:

BT = 4 (a small shot at fame and a chance to embarrass yourself nationally)

R   = 2 (long-term reward: "Hey . . . aren't you that idiot who was in that movie?")

WT = 98 (broken bones, paralysis, or other serious injury)

A   = 10 (You would likely recover but have some lingering pains and the footage to prove it.)

L   = 60% (of serious injury)

P   = 10% (Helmets, pads, and a positive attitude can help only so much.)

Best-case equation: $4 + 2 = 6$

Worst-case equation: $(98 - 10) \times (.60 - .10) = 44$

$6 < 44$

Analysis: Keep your feet on the ground, pal.

Don't you wish all of life's decisions were as easy to make?

Defining Your Own Terms

Of course, the values you put into these equations are subjective and personal, so this isn't an exact science. Don't use this formula as a final authority for your life planning. Yet, the formula and the process of identifying and quantifying the variables of your decision are intended to help you remove the emotional restraints that govern your approach to uncertainty. There are some situations in which the potential negative outcome is so unacceptable that we need to walk away, even if the likelihood of it occurring is small. Other times, we can push our personal envelope to try things when the likelihood of failure or the perception of risk is enormous. Just remember to consider these components: What is the best thing that can happen? What is the worst? What are your odds? Are you willing to accept the risk in order to enjoy the potential rewards?

When I first attempted unicycle riding, I knew that the likelihood of failure was initially 100 percent. You don't learn to ride a unicycle without falling off . . . a lot. So, the skinned and banged-up knees, hands, and elbows, coupled with many hours of frustration, were a foregone conclusion. But for me, the potential rewards, the best-case scenario, was tremendously enticing. I seriously wanted to master this skill so that I could incorporate it in my performances, show off for friends, and simply navigate the neighborhood in style. I saw the muscled legs of unicycle experts, and I wanted a pair of those, too!

So, I sought out the experts and asked how I could best learn. They gave me some great tips to inform my preparation and increase the likelihood of success:

- Start with a class.
- Use good equipment.
- Learn how to fall, then how to ride.
- Find a support system (in my case, it was my neighbor's fence along the alley behind our Chicago home).
- Don't give up—the breakthrough moment happens when you least expect it.
- Continue to lean forward, even when you are struggling, and pedal like you mean it.

Good rules for unicycling. Great rules for life.

You are ready to lean forward, express your commitment, and begin the journey. This doesn't mean you have it all figured out yet. It does mean, however, that you are going from the hypothetical scenario of having an idea to the tangible reality of becoming your expressed desire. Because when you are learning forward, you have

Heightened focus and determination. Your senses and your commitment will both be sharpened.

Increased credibility. People take you seriously because you are not just a dreamer, you are a doer.

Real-world experience. Classroom knowlege is no match for unabashed feedback.

Momentum. Once you are already engaged in doing, it's easier to continue doing.

When you lean forward, into the unknown or around an unexpected turn, don't do it timidly. Accelerate through the changes, twists, and bumps.

As Einstein's First Law of Motion states: Bodies in motion tend to stay in motion. Bodies at rest tend to stay at rest. I believe that applies to human bodies, too. So take a deep breath, lean forward, and go!

13

LEVERAGE YOUR RESOURCES

AT THE END of the previous chapter, you were left "leaning forward"—off balance—in midair and in motion toward a desirable destination on your six-foot unicycle. If this resembles your current life situation, as many people tell me it does, then you understand both the excitement and the uncertainty that go along with bold action.

But once you affect this off-balance posture, once you lean forward on your personal "unicycle," a new and immediate goal becomes crystal clear: avoid crashing to the ground! To move forward and circumvent the crash, you instinctively realize that two things need to happen fast. You need to pedal and steer! In other words, use your physical and mental resources in an intelligent and efficient manner.

When we are pedaling, we are using our physical resources: Show up. Work hard. Invest your time and money. Execute your plan. Perform your daily disciplines. Sometimes pedaling literally translates to manual labor, using your body to exert effort for a meaningful purpose and tangible result. The gratification that comes from pedaling forward can be immense when you glance back over your shoulder to see how far you have come.

But by itself, pedaling is insufficient and can produce mixed results. Are you pedaling in the right direction? Are you pedaling uphill or downhill? Are you taking the most established, well-worn path, or is there a better way to go that will save you time and make the journey more interesting? These questions highlight how we "steer" the course, which requires us to make good use of our mental resources: imagination, creativity, strategic thinking, seeking advice and direction from others, and asking intelligent questions.

When you are on purpose, you mysteriously attract new resources to aid your efforts—and discover better ways to use what you already possess.

With the Right Leverage . . .

The title of this chapter, and the fourth step of the OBOP process, is not "Use Your Resources." Sure, a commitment to use what you have is certainly important. It sure beats the alternative—letting your gifts, skills, and opportunities sit on the shelf and whither away. But mere "use" is an insufficient objective; there are many ways to use your resources. The question is, are you expending effort in a way that delivers the greatest possible returns? Are you gaining maximum leverage from your energy and action?

Your resources include your skills, relationships, money, time, energy, reputation, experiences (both successes and hardships), ideas, questions, and answers. We all have these resources. Some areas are strong, others may be lacking. But the key question is: Do you gain the fullest benefit from what you already possess? And the answer, for most of us, is: Probably not. There is always some way to tune up your engine of achievement and get more streamlined and powerful performance.

Some resources are limited or restricted, but many wonderful resources are available to you and me, free of charge. One example: the public library. Nothing is stopping us from taking advantage of this incredible asset. Simply walk in to a local branch and leverage the tremendous resources waiting for you—books on every subject, audio programs, DVDs, movies, educational programs, guest speakers, and access to a quiet, clean, and comfortable work space.

When you apply what you have in a way that combines creative thought with connected purpose and deliberate action, you gain tremendous leverage.

My definition of leverage in this context means you are able to gain additional power through the intelligent application of force or, in other words, by taking strategic action. It is a way of coordinating and combining your skills, your relationships, your energy, your time, and your other resources so that they feed off of one another. And the greatest leverage comes from connecting your purpose directly to the resources available, gaining greater meaning and value from the assets of your life. With enough leverage, you can accomplish anything.

Archimedes of Syracuse, the Greek mathematition, physicist, inventor, and engineer, expressed this very idea: "Give me a place to stand and with a lever I will move the whole world."

When Archimedes spoke these words (more than two hundred years BC), I don't think he meant them as hyberbole. I take this notion literally. With enough leverage, our ideas and actions can move the world: move others to action; transform beliefs about what is possible; swipe away doubt and destructive ideas; give birth to new possibilities; shift perceptions, attitudes, and reality; and create opporunities that never before existed.

The question is really "*How* do you wish to move the world?" What is your mission? Your purpose? There is something you and only you are here on Earth to do. If you turn away from this task, electing not to "move the world," then the world suffers for it and your life becomes an unfinished symphony.

Which Comes First, the Lean or the Lever?

Sometimes I am asked, "Don't you have these steps out of order?" Some people think that you should figure out the "leverage your resources" step before you "lean forward." After all, why would you throw yourself into uncertainty and start falling without first deciding exactly what you are going to do and how you were going to best use your resources? Fair question, and it certainly ressonates with many people. Perhaps even you. Yet, I wholeheartedly believe that you should lean forward first, that it is the most powerful way to for you to succeed. Here's why.

You can always be a little more ready, prepared, or informed before deciding to take action and lean forward. But at some point, and far sooner than you might realize, the act of "getting ready" to act becomes a stalling tactic. And once you indulge inaction, your stall may manifest into something far more debilitating: fear.

I'm not asking you to leap blindly into the abyss without any preparation. I'm saying you are already prepared. First of all, you are completely cognizant of your situation and your environment; you own your reality. This first critical step ensures that you meet the challenge as it exists—not better or worse. You have identified your strengths, weaknesses, resources, and limitations. You know what you have to work with.

You've sought and found your purpose, determining exactly what you want and why it is so important to you. With this step, you connected to a powerful force that will sustain and inform you. Indeed, the fulcrum of purpose is the greatest leverage you can possess.

You don't need an exact plan for how you will leverage your resources in order to take action. And I would argue that, in many situations, you do need to take action before you understand how to best leverage your resources. The application of additional force, energy, and resources, if it is well timed and judged, will allow you to harness the moment and enjoy the ride of your life.

Creating Leverage

I can sense what you are thinking. Great concept, but how do you do it? How can I more effectively leverage my resources? Well, here are seven practical ideas you can begin using right now.

NARROW YOUR FOCUS

When you have a general sense of what you want, you may have a warm and fuzzy feeling. Examples of broad, general desires include:

- "I just want to be happy."

- "I just want to make enough money so I don't have to worry about it."

- "I really need to get in shape."

These are ambiguous ambitions. They may be well intentioned, but they have no leverage. They are easy to wiggle out of. The motivating factor for achievement, the purpose behind the goal, has been watered down with generalities.

By contrast, when you use undiluted, concentrated purpose, and specific, narrow targets, you engage powerful internal and external forces to materialize your desire. Sometimes this happens as a result of your persistent effort, which can only be sustained with a narrow focus. Other times, the forces at work are far more mysterious. I believe that when you are absolutely sure of what you want, the Universe, or God, or the Law of Attraction—call it what you wish—will deliver.

Let's restate the earlier desires within a specific, narrow framework:

- "I will be grateful every day for what I have. I will share joy and positivity with others wherever I go." If you do that, trust me, you'll be happy.

- "I will pay off my mortgage in five years." Now that's a specific goal. You don't have to know exactly how it will happen yet. But know, with certainty, what you want to happen.

- "I will lose ten pounds and be able to run five miles in forty-five minutes." Okay! Now you know what you're working for. Go for it!

Notice that the generalities all were characterized by "I want" or "I need," but the narrowed focus forced a change to "I will." Those two words provide amazing leverage to achievement, and they are yours to use free of charge.

ENGAGE YOUR LIFE SPHERES

We covered this in depth in part 2 of this book, so I won't take much time again here. But let me restate that when you strengthen your lifelines and find multiple reasons to achieve what you want, you accelerate your forward progress dramatically. You gain leverage. Instead of viewing a challenge or opportunity as an isolated event that you somehow need to find time to address, figure out, and conquer, see it as it truly is—connected to all five spheres of your life. Make supercharged choices and reap the multiplied rewards. Get creative, and use all five of your life spheres to get maximum leverage.

MOLD A MAGNETIC VISION

In order to engage the power of attraction, you need to become more magnetic. Think and speak about your life and your future in a way that is not only specific but also emotionally charged. When you describe what you are working on, to yourself and to others, you need to feel it, like a kid on Christmas morning. Connect to the reason why you want it—the purpose that propels you forward—and share the excitement.

There is so much uncertainty in the world and so many people who are reluctant to express what they want and believe. Consequently, when you become confident about your plan, purpose, and possibilities (instead of detractors and doubts), your presence alone satisfies an unfulfilled need in the lives of those around you. It's contagious as well. Your enthusiasm and vision will spread like wildfire, first to the people you encounter and then into other lives and circumstances outside your view.

Be prepared. Your magnetism will also attract some skeptics who seem challenged by your confidence and view. Positive forces attract negative forces—it's a fact. Just treat the skeptics with kindness and gratitude, then continue to stay steeped in your vision of the transformation that is coming to your life and to the people you serve. Positivity, combined with persistence, will prevail.

EXPLOIT YOUR GREATEST STRENGTHS

The word *exploit* may bring to mind some negative connotations. It has become synonymous with taking an unfair or selfish advantage of a circumstance or opportunity. The meaning I intend, however, is purely positive.

In chapter 10, "Own Your Reality," you identified your strengths—the attributes and resources you have in plentiful supply. These strengths encompass the skills that come naturally to you and the activities and pursuits that bring you joy and satisfaction. To create unstoppable leverage and propel yourself forward, seek to discover ways to exploit your natural source of abundance. In other words, take full advantage of what you possess. Harness your gifts and use them in a targeted and high-impact manner.

For example, let's say your gift is communication. You enjoy talking with others in person and over the telephone. The ability to converse with and persuade others comes naturally to you. Great! You have a valuable gift. You could choose to use this gift in various ways. You could, for instance, become a telemarketer who spends hour after hour talking with strangers over the phone in an attempt to sell some product or service. That would, after all, be a way to use your natural abilities. But is it the best way? Probably (and hopefully) not.

To better leverage, or exploit, your communication talents, you could apply the same amount of force (personal effort) into something that brings you a more meaningful challenge, greater possible satisfaction, or increased rewards. For instance, you could use the same skills (communication and persuasion) to be a successful salesperson in a profitable and meaningful enterprise: one that excites you—perhaps even your own business. Or, taking an entirely different route, you might lend your talents to a meaningful cause, such as encouraging at-risk youth or promoting a worthy charity or some other important personal cause. The point is, you can spend the same amount of effort and time and create multiplied rewards if you are willing to exploit your strengths.

In any professional pursuit, there are those who are excellent—truly gifted—but never seem to break into the next level of success. Sadly, they might become frustrated or lose interest, choosing, ultimately, to abandon their gift because it "wasn't enough" to sustain them or facilitate the right opportunity. Or maybe they just weren't able to find the right application of their talents to gain adequate leverage.

The word *exploit*, as a noun, means "a bold and daring feat." To use your abilities in a nontraditional way is bold and daring. It takes a certain amount of nerve to value your strengths and bring them to a new arena, one that may be unfamiliar to you.

I knew from an early age that I could juggle, do backflips, and entertain audiences. But let's face it; these skills are really glorified "party tricks." I was able to leverage my talents to earn money, meet interesting people, travel, build a business, and even pay for my college education. Not bad. But was it the greatest exploitation of my strengths and abilities? I didn't think so.

While it was unclear exactly what I should be doing, I sensed that there was another application of my skills that could bring about enhanced opportunities and, more important, tap into a higher-level purpose for my life—the next evolution of who I was and what I did. It meant taking my performance to a different market, one that was unfamiliar to me, and delivering more than I had in the past. In order to transform, I would have to find another ingredient that would allow me to create a new offering— one that excited me as well as my audience.

CREATE A NEW SYNTHESIS

For me, the missing "ingredient" was right in front of me—a natural thirst for motivation and a desire to share a positive message with others. I was raised by positive parents who instilled in me a strong work ethic as well as an understanding about the connection among attitude, beliefs, and life events. In college, I became a student of such speakers and authors as Zig Ziglar, Anthony Robbins, Wayne Dyer, Brian Tracy, and others. I always had an audio program in my car and would listen to these great thinkers on my trips to performances.

After graduating, I was looking for the next evolution of my performance career. My shows were well received and highly regarded by booking agents, but I was losing interest in doing the "same old thing." At the time, I didn't think about "leveraging my talents," but that's exactly what happened.

When I made the decision to combine my performances with my desire to share a message, I created something new. Suddenly, I was reenergized by my performance career. I once again felt the excitement and trepidation before showtime that had subsided through the years of performing. What once was familiar became new again—for me and my audiences—and the result was the discovery of my personal passion and a career that remains immensely rewarding.

By synthesizing my peformance talents with professional speaking, I found a greater leverage for my skills than I could ever enjoy with either pursuit on its own. Similarly, you can gain added oomph from your skills by seeking new combinations of your resources or creative applications of your talents.

PURSUE A PARTNERSHIP

In addition to exploiting your strengths, you will also need to shore up your weaknesses and vulnerabilities. I see this often with performers who are fantastic on stage but lack an understanding about how to run the "business" that goes along with their "show." Both parts are important, of course. To neglect vital aspects (because they are uninteresting or less natural) is an incomplete devotion to our craft. We need to acknowledge and address areas of improvement.

Another way to supplement your strengths, however, is to develop a partnership with someone whose natural abilities complement and complete yours. If you pursue excellence, you will attract others who share your vision. Excellence attracts excellence. You never know who's in your audience, which is why it is always important to extend your best effort and express your deeply held desires. Your passion and commitment to excellence will draw like-minded people into your realm, and often these individuals will possess information or abilities that provide the missing puzzle piece you've been seeking.

Ask for help. The most successful and happiest people are those who have learned that they do not have to do it alone. When you exhibit a willingness to put forth your own effort, you earn the respect of others and increase the likelihood that they will be willing to support you. When you share your purpose in a clear and compelling way, you will be amazed at the support you can marshal and the resources you can attract.

Help others. What do you have to offer the world? What is the most helpful way to deliver it to one person, or to many? In what way do your resources provide the greatest benefit to those around you? When you help others, you ultimately receive more of what you desire.

MANAGE AND MANUFACTURE ENERGY

You cannot manufacture more time in your day, but you can create more energy. Leverage is about efficiency and thoughtful application of resources. Start mastering this skill by learning to manage your most vital resource—your personal energy level. Don't waste physical or mental energy on unimportant or destructive issues. Add fuel to your reserves by exercising, eating healthy foods, and drinking lots of water. Make the best of rest, and understand that when you allow yourself sufficient sleep, you are being productive. You are producing energy, promoting healing, and allowing your subconscious mind the opportunity to work out ideas and solve problems. Take pauses at key moments to focus your thoughts and to breathe; you'll rebound with greater resilience. Be selective about the way you choose to invest your internal power.

Even when your resources may be woefully depleted, they are not exhausted; there is always something you can do. When you are shaken or thrown dramatically off your game plan, honestly assess what you do have to work with, and then take the next purposeful, positive action.

Discover your resources. Build on your strengths. Strengthen your weaknesses both by improving your skills and by building relationships with people who complement your talents with theirs. Then put those resources into action with a direct connection to your purpose, and experience the leverage that comes from knowing what you want, why you want it, and what you have (your resources) to aid in the journey.

You Are Attractive

This isn't a come on, or even a compliment. It's a fact. You attract the circumstances, qualities, and outcomes you think about. What you value and imagine on a daily basis becomes the next chapter of your story. Be careful what you think—today's imaginings become tomorrow's reality.

The greatest resource you have is your mind. You leverage your brain power through the discipline of controlled and consistent thought, which is why "seeking your purpose" is not a one-time event. It is a perpetual necessity. You are always steering. Regularly remind yourself what you want and why you want it. Envision successful outcomes from your plans and projects. Permit yourself to dream big dreams, and provide details for the design of your destiny.

When you are in this mind-set, imagining and free thinking about your future, resist the temptation to drift into logical rationales. You may undermine yourself by concluding that your dreams can't possibly happen. Or at the very least, your rational mind will scale back the plans to a bite-size version of your fantasy. Don't do it! There is a time for logic and a time for creative thought. Dare to dream big and you'll be amazed how the forces in this world, seen and unseen, applaud and accommodate your efforts.

The key to leveraging all your resources, including your mind, is to remain flexible. Be committed to an outcome, but stay open to the path that will take you there. It rarely resembles the journey you intended. Persist in being both pliant and curious about how your vision may come about.

I'm a golfer. I love the game: the solitude, the challenge, and the satisfaction that comes from playing. I try to play once a week, which is not always possible with my schedule. But I continue to dream about shooting low scores and playing some of the world's best courses. To support this dream, I've fashioned an eighteen-hole "yard golf" course in my yard. The "holes" are various objects, including strategically positioned rocks, the metal cable box that protrudes from my lawn, a tree trunk, my air-conditioning unit, etc., and I use practice balls that fly only about forty yards to protect my and my neighbors' windows. The course is complete with water hazards, elevation changes, and blind drives. And the best part—you can complete a round in about twenty-five minutes.

But to make the course complete, I needed a putting green. Two of my major hurdles: putting greens are expensive, and my wife was far from sold on the idea. So I figured if I could leverage my resources to manufacture an opportunity to make this happen at a reasonable cost, she could be persuaded.

I targeted a company based in Georgia and approached the CEO with a proposition. I sent him all of my marketing materials, a copy of my book, and a DVD featuring segments from my speech. I told him that I wanted to deliver a program for (or on behalf of) his organization, and in exchange for my usual fee, I would accept a "barter" arrangement. A great plan, I thought—my speech (and maybe some product thrown in to sweeten the deal) in exchange for a putting green.

He liked my stuff. But the problem was that he didn't really have a need for a speaker. They had never hired a speaker for their company or sponsored an event, so he didn't see it happening right away. But because I had a vision, I would not be deterred. He just needed to be persuaded. So I continued calling, writing, and sending various products and promotional items. I was persistent to the point of annoying. This went on for more than a year.

Then something inexplicable happened. Another, much larger, company called me. They actually manufacture the turf that the previous company resells. They're the best in the business when it comes to synthetic sports surfaces. And they called me with a proposition.

"We're having a company meeting and an associate of mine heard you speak and told me you were excellent. We'd love to have you speak for our event, but we don't have a big budget. Would you consider speaking for a reduced fee if we could work out some sort of trade? I understand you're a golfer . . ."

You guessed it. I now have a putting green in my backyard. It looks just like I imagined it, but it came about in a way I never expected. As I leveraged my resources to get to a solution, I attracted a better alternative. Some would say that this is a coincidence. But I don't think so. I think that the thought and effort I invested in my original plan somehow attracted the other opportunity.

Thought is a powerful resource. But thought combined with action is undeniable. Your actions express your intentions and invite unseen forces to validate and accommodate your desires.

Be committed to the outcome but open to changing your process for getting there, because it will always be different from what you first imagined.

You attract what you envision. Your thoughts will bring about ideas and opportunities. But unless you act upon your thoughts and leverage your resources, you will fail to capitalize on the full measure of your attractiveness.

We are all given a multitude of gifts throughout our lifetime. These come in many forms and include, among others: talents, skills, relationships, insights, dreams, opportunities, and lessons learned from hardships. As we evolve from the people we are to the people we wish to become, these are the resources we must apply. The quest for the greatest leverage, or application of what you have, begins with willingness. When you become open to change for a purposeful reason, you will discover the means to pedal and steer your way forward. But the decision to continue and complete the transformation is a daily choice.

14

FOLLOW THROUGH

THE REAL JOY of accomplishment is not only to complete a task but also to finish it with excitement and excellence.

As we reach the last chapter of this book together, the finish line is finally within sight. In fact, we are so close to the end now, we have nearly absorbed the complete scope and benefit of the process We reason that it's almost as good *as finishing*, and the temptation to skim, skip, or move on to the next book, task, or obligation may begin to creep into your psyche (or into mine) and eliminate the possibility of completion.

One thing's for sure. If I don't finish this book, there is absolutely no chance you will.

Off balance on purpose is more than a philosophy—it's a process of self-expansion toward your infinite potential. And the fifth and perhaps most critical step is follow through. This thought may seem like an obvious notion, hardly even worth mentioning. I will tell you, however, that this is the most overlooked and undervalued aspect to positive change. Untold numbers of dreams are lost; countless heartfelt desires are abandoned; the positive transformations of millions of lives are unrealized, all because of a failure to follow through.

"Close" is not good enough. "Nearly there" is a million miles from completion. It's the difference between everything and nothing. Will you attain your conquest? Will you at last reap the ultimate benefit of all of your previous efforts? Or will all of those efforts be wasted, diminished, and made irrelevant because of your inability to finish what you started?

That is the choice you and I must make when we are confronted by the inevitable surprises that materialize when we are on the final turn of our marathon race. What you expected would be an unfettered victory lap now suddenly appears to include double-high hurdles, lengthy detours, and even a long jump over a pit of hungry crocodiles. Screw that! I've come this far, and I'm spent. Exhausted! I've given everything I have to this project, and now it looks like the last-minute setbacks will demolish the whole effort. Oh well, I've done the best I can. What do I get for second place? What if I just ride my momentum to the finish line?

Coasting to Completion

"Are we there yet?" comes the familiar, whiny question from the child in the backseat. The road trip has been punishing for offspring and parents alike, and both parties wish only for it to end.

"We're nearly there. Stop asking!"

When we are nearly there, wherever "there" may be, it is often at the end of a supreme effort. We are physically and mentally exhausted. We are less than our best. We feel that our momentum alone, generated by the previous work completed, will be sufficient to carry us to the end.

It is not. Yield to the temptation to "coast to completion" and you will have effectively compromised and diminished all of your previous hard work. Don't sell yourself short. Follow through with a renewed commitment, and know that the conclusion of your conquest will demand your best abilities.

The last 5 percent. The last 2 percent. The last 1 percent of any job is often the hardest. Usually, it is also the most critical. Always, it is more involved and time-consuming than we had imagined. That's because, before a project begins, we don't generally understand all of the details involved with the final push. Sure, in our visualizations we picture the end result—the attainment of our goal. The prize. We also gravitate toward considering the enormity of the challenges—the 98 percent that will take us almost to the finish line. But as we approach the finish line, we are often exhausted, anxious for completion, and ready to move on.

As you get within striking distance of being done, a few paces from completion, something bizarre happens. The finish line moves. Really, it does. It recedes into the distance, obscured by new, unanticipated details and things that must be done, all of which stand between you and victory. It takes endurance and a disciplined effort to sustain the commitment for the duration, to overcome the unanticipated elements, and finally to attain completion.

It's a matter of perspective. What we think is the last 2 percent may actually be the last 10 percent. We don't really know, especially if it is a project we haven't done before, or a race we've never run. For me, this was absolutely the case when I wrote and published my first book. For two years I kept saying "It's almost finished."Two years! And I actually believed it was almost finished. I hadn't written a book before and didn't completely understand all of the intricate details involved in the final process: Edits upon edits, layout, graphic design, printer selection, figuring out where to store the copies.

In the end, it all comes down to quality control. I could have quit and called the race complete. But then all of my previous efforts would have fallen short of their potential. What I had to realize was that producing the best possible product was far more important than my self-imposed and uninformed deadline. And the setbacks that materialized during the "home stretch" were some of the most trying aspects of the entire process.

Trials and Traps

In Paulo Coelho's inspiring book *The Alchemist*, the sage and wizened title character teaches his disciple, the story's hero, that

> Before a dream is realized, the Soul of the World tests every-
> thing that was learned along the way. It does this not because
> it is evil, but so we can, in addition to realizing our dreams,

master the lessons we've learned as we've moved toward that dream. That's the point at which most people give up. It's the point at which, as we say in the language of the desert, "one dies of thirst when the palm trees have appeared on the horizon." Every search begins with beginner's luck, and every search ends with the victor's being severely tested.

When we strike out on a bold quest, throwing ourselves off balance in pursuit of a greater purpose, we engage powerful forces to propel and aid us. But as we approach victory, we will be tested by the traps that befall us. And the most severe trials are usually reserved for the final chapters.

What stops us from following through? This enemy has two faces in the form of two types of traps we encounter: those that are set before us, and those we set ourselves.

The obstacles set before us include unexpected events, economic downturns, naysayers, rivals, and well-meaning people who simply don't share our vision. In the face of negative influences and uninvited distractions, we are challenged to remain connected to the purpose behind our pursuit and envision a successful outcome, even in the face of adversity. The heroes and heroines who attain their personal triumph are those who rise above these external challenges, slay the dragons in their path, and persist until the storm subsides to reveal them victorious.

The traps set by us are perhaps even more destructive, due to their insidious nature. In this case, the enemy we are fighting is a traitor, a double agent, who works in the shadows of our thinking and patiently waits for our weakest moments to do its evil business. This is the dastardly villain who, while pretending to be on our side, wields the weapons of doubt and distraction to sabotage our success. This villain's methods are cunning and stealthlike, often disguised as comfort and consolation. But do not be fooled. Expose this rapscallion, even as it is proved to be you.

DOUBT

We become our worst enemy when we indulge our doubts and fears. When we say "Who am I to think myself worthy?" or "This dream just isn't possible.

Forget it and be content with what you have," we lay treacherous traps. Now, don't misunderstand. To have these thoughts is natural, especially when we are at low moments. But to give them credence or let them slip by unnoticed is unacceptable.

When you have self-doubts or become fearful, do not ignore them or simply dismiss them as unimportant. Recognize those thoughts as poisonous, and then treat them at once with a potent and powerful antidote. Reconnect to your purpose and the meaning of your quest. Read something that inspires you. Reach out to a role model and ask him or her to help you persevere. At these times, you need a new thought that will enable you to take the next step forward, such as:

- "I've come this far, and I'm not about to give up now."
- "I've prepared for this moment all of my life. Of course I'm ready."
- "I deserve to be the fullest measure of my potential."
- "Dream big. Take action. Follow through!"
- "I may be off balance, but I'm definitely on purpose."

DISTRACTION

Another tactic we unwittingly employ is distraction, which I first discussed in chapter 3. I confess to you that this is my nemesis. I believe that if I ever submitted to the diagnosis, I would quickly become the "poster boy" for Adult Attention Deficit Disorder. I don't say that lightly, or to diminish those with this condition. My wife, my staff, my friends, and my kids would all back me up on this point. My mind works in free-association mode rather than linear functionality. I've been blessed by abundant energy that promotes perpetual motion. I can become stir crazy in a matter of moments and find myself in need of physical activity to channel my energy. I'll frequently walk around my office, stretch, or head outside for a quick nine holes of yard golf. Granted, I've used these characteristics to my advantage, especially to create and deliver energized speaking presentations.

When I am completely absorbed in what I am doing, I have no problem with attention. This comes out in my workouts, practice sessions, and certainly when I am performing. But leading up to those moments, I am inclined to entertain and submit to distractions, often to my detriment.

Distractions, like all productivity traps, come in two types—those that come at you and those you yourself create. The first set includes events, people, and situations that arise unexpectedly and interrupt you. These external sources demand that you handle them urgently, or at least entertain them long enough to disrupt whatever you were previously doing.

The other sort of distractions are a form of self-destruction. We ourselves create them. When the mind wanders off the task at hand and latches onto an unrelated idea or another important project, it becomes far more difficult to follow through with what we are doing. Entertain one distraction, and you must consider them all! How else would you be able to distinguish which ones are more important than your work and which are not? How in the world do you make those decisions?

What I have learned and applied to combat my own disposition toward diversion is that the root cause of succumbing to either type—externally or internally generated distractions—is identical. We become distracted when we allow other things to become more important than what we are doing. It comes down to personal responsibility. Distractions can distract us only if we let them; otherwise, they are just part of the "noise" of life, which we can disregard while we remain focused on following through with what matters most.

This is easier said than done, yet we can employ certain tactics to minimize the unwelcome distractions from subverting our efforts and filibustering our follow through.

Make it important—Intensify and acknowlege the importance of what you are doing and why it is essential that you finish the task with excellence. If you are having difficulty sustaining an effort to completion, perhaps the job or learning process isn't as meaningful as you think it is. Examine your motives and explore what is at stake if you do not follow through. Then, if you determine that this is really important, make it so! Own the unstoppable drive that will propel you to the finish line.

Express yourself—When other people hear you talk about why your projects are so important, they will be less likely to distract you. Much of what you think of right now as unwelcome disruptions can be neutralized by proclaiming the importance and need for completion. When you have a mission, other people will help you or will get out of your way.

Keep your schedule—I'm not advocating that you be totally focused and unavailable to outside influences 24/7. That would be unhealthy, and the other spheres of your life would likely suffer due to your maniacal devotion. Determine which time is the best for you to attack your challenge with high energy and a focused mind (for me, writing in the mornings, before my kids wake up, is best) and then stay within those time constraints.

You'll find that two things happen: (1) Distractions will wait for you, because your postponement is finite, and clearly you are doing something important. (2) The time you spend working will be more productive. When you schedule the time for action, instead of saying "I'll get around to this. It's one of many things on my list," you create a window of opportunity for powerful productivity. You will spend less time "getting ready" and will be more likely to "get busy" because you've determined that this is the appointed hour for action.

Claim your space—When it is time to keep your appointment with your important tasks, shut your door and create a physical barrier from distractions. Or, if this doesn't work, go to another space where you know you will not be interrupted. It doesn't cost a dime to go to a library to work, and the quiet atmosphere may help you focus.

Enforce rules—What are the rules you need to make and enforce in order to stay focused and impervious to distractions? When I am writing, for example, I know that if I stop my progress to check email, for even a moment, I have just ended my writing session. In an instant, I become sucked into the thoughts of others and the game of deciding which emails are important and which are not. This thought process stops my creativity in its tracks, breaks my concentration, and diminishes the importance of what I was previously doing.

It is very difficult for me to get back into the writing zone at that point and rekindle the "magic." So, my rules include: No emails. No phone calls (that's easy, as most of my writing takes place between 5:00 and 7:00 a.m.).

No Web surfing, except to look up references and ideas related to my work. It is such a small window of time, and such a huge project, I simply cannot allow myself to break the rules. Plus, I know I will still have the entire day to take care of those other items on my list of things to do.

Following Through with Others

Imagine your favorite baseball player swinging with unbridled effort and connecting with the "perfect pitch." The sound of the contact—the "crack" of bat on ball—sends an immediate thrill through the stadium and a simultaneous chill down the spines of the defenders. But what makes the ball fly out of the park? It's not the initial contact. It's the follow through. Ask any swing coach, and he will tell you that the power comes from the extension, the subtle roll of the wrists, and the acceleration and rotation of the bat through a wide arc—a full range of motion. Home runs happen because of follow through.

Apply the same principle when you "step up to the plate" and take your swings at the fastballs, curveballs, and sliders of life. Full extension—complete follow through—will increase your "batting percentage" and ensure the greatest liklihood that your projects and tasks are completed correctly on the first attempt.

But to extend the baseball analogy a little further, consider that most of the situations you encounter in life are not solo undertakings, but team efforts. We rely on others to help us. We depend on people to perform their job tasks and fulfill their responsibilities. Often, we have just one attempt—a very limited opportunity—to express what we need, explain what we want, or inspire our teammates (and fans) to see our vision of what is possible. When you really need to get your point across and enlist the support and assistance of others, it takes far more than solid contact. It takes follow through.

That's why advertising campaigns for popular products, services, and companies don't just send a single message to a mass audience. They find a variety of ways to reinforce that message, and then they launch a sustained effort, a comprehensive campaign, that repeats their message in a variety of creative ways, evoking the interest and emotion of their audience. Politicians do likewise, restating their beliefs and ideas (often ad nauseum) through various channels and in multiple speeches, until their message becomes repeatable, powerful, and universally understood. They don't stop campaigning until election day.

Implement the following guidelines to ensure that your interactions and communication attempts have maximum follow through and impact.

Express yourself with confidence—People will register your passion before they will hear your message. When you speak with someone and attempt to persuade them, be sure of what you believe and say it with sincerity, enthusiasm, and conviction.

Express yourself completely and concisely—At first these may seem like competing objectives, but in truth this is the essence of effective communication. When your message is so crisp and concentrated that it can be related quickly, it will be heard, understood, and repeated. Find the shortest distance (the fewest words) to reach your audience, and you will turbocharge your communication.

Use multiple "channels"—Say it well, say it quickly, and say it in a variety of ways. As a conversation develops, look for different ways to convey your ideas: engaging examples, descriptive words, and emotional connections. People "tune in" to different channels depending on their point of reference, their personal experience, and their existing beliefs. Communication is not one size fits all. Adapt and explore new possibilities.

Confirm understanding—The biggest mistake or failure to follow through is the assumption that we've understood or been understood. We tend to assume that people know what we know and think as we do, and therefore, we may stop short of completely transferring our ideas. It is essential that you stop talking, ask questions, and listen to your audience.

Reconnect and refresh—Revisit a past conversation and follow up with the person you spoke with. Ask questions about how things have progressed since you last spoke. Review the key points about what you covered and offer additional insights and updates. By taking this extra step, you establish yourself as an ongoing, interested partner.

Calling Your Own Endings

When it comes to following through, you are the person who ultimately decides when you are done. You may be responsible to others for the work you produce. Often, you are given certain parameters and the associated time frames. But ultimately, you are the one who determines when a task, process, or project is complete. You are the one who has to call the ending.

Calling the ending is a bold move. It means announcing that the work is over, the project is complete. Finished. Finalized. You're done. You can now enjoy the satisfaction of accomplishment and then move your attention and energy in another direction. It is a joyous, liberating moment, but it can be hard to reach, especially if you are a perfectionist or creative thinker.

> My mother, Diana Thurmon, is a sensational artist. In her forty-plus-year career, she has produced thousands of paintings in a wide variety of styles. Her artwork is in demand, widely respected, and enjoyed by people all over the country. How did she do it? Answer: One painting at a time. When my mom gets to work creating a new piece of artwork, she immerses herself in the effort. She works quickly, guided by instinct and curiosity. She moves forward without second-guessing her brushstrokes or imposing self-restraints. She gives all of her creative efforts and artistic talents to the task at hand, adding details, extra touches, and characteristics that make the painting come alive in her own original style. But once she reaches the moment when she feels the effort is complete, she signs the painting, sets down the brush, and steps away from the canvas. It's done.
>
> Of course, before the paint dries, she has probably started envisioning the next painting. There's a lot more inspiration to tap. But this painting is complete. It represents a snapshot in time and captures the full extent of her creative effort.

I think we can all benefit from an approach to our own creative projects that views them as snapshots in time—a collection of choices and actions as applied to a specific challenge. The way you handle a task or question today is determined by your perspective, skills, capabilities, and outlook. Those factors will evolve and shift over time. A year from now (or five . . . or ten), you will look back at today's challenges and remark at how you handled them, perhaps thinking you would do that differently now. But the point is you did it! You handled it. You followed through.

A familiar phrase I often keep in mind is "Finished is better than perfect." This reminds me to keep the end in mind. With a view toward completion, I am also eager to fully apply myself—physically and mentally—to whatever task I am facing. I strive to get it done, and get it done right.

To have an unfinished piece of work, no matter how good it may be, is almost like not having it at all. It's also a selfish act to hold on to something you have created. Release your ideas and creations. Share them with the world, and allow others to benefit from knowing and experiencing what you have to offer.

GOING TO ELEVEN

When you call your own endings, you also determine the level of excellence, the attention to detail, the amount of effort you will apply to the challenge at hand. Those factors will determine your results as well as your reputation. So, how do you wish to be viewed? I think there are two distinct (and sometimes competing) qualities a true achiever strives for: Get it right. Get it done.

Get it right—Getting it right means that you consistently produce quality thoughts and results. You don't always go for the easiest answer or outcome. You are willing to take another step beyond where others may typically stop. I call this "going to eleven." If "start to finish" is a scale of one to ten, then go to eleven. Go just a little farther than others would have, and you will stand out by far. More important, this attitude will help you get past the trials and traps that crop up as you near the finish line. Depending on your project, going to eleven may involve an extra layer of thought, a few choice details, and a level of execution that goes beyond the ordinary. Assuming that quality is there, the extra touches will make your previous efforts shine and make the end result uniquely you. And when you get it right, you define how the project ends.

Get it done—Sometimes the "finish line" is ambiguous or undetermined, especially if you are blazing a new path. Some projects and most creative undertakings are like this. No matter how much time, preparation, effort, and thought you have invested, you can always find something else to improve. It can be tempting to continue to fine-tune every aspect of your project, add extra touches, rethink, and rework various components.

Be careful. Left unchecked, these efforts can become stalling techniques which may or may not improve the end result in any appreciable way. While tenacity and attention to detail are admirable qualities, there comes a point in every project to finish tweaking and tinkering.

DOES THIS PROJECT MAKE MY BUTT LOOK BIG?

Sometimes we need another person's opinion when we contemplate the size of our end . . . or our ending. When you are immersed in a project for an extended period of time, you can easily lose your objectivity. In order to follow through, you might benefit from a fresh perspective. Sometimes calling our own endings means that we enlist the help of others who can offer a different viewpoint. Ask for their input, but do so in a manner that is aimed at completion. In other words, you want their opinion, but you are not willing to start over and rework major aspects of this project. Instead of asking "What do you think?" you might ask a targeted question, such as, "What do I need to resolve or handle in order to bring this to a strong conclusion?"

Select someone you respect who is also qualified to provide useful feedback. Once you have received their input, decide to incorporate it and use it to propel you to the finish. Or if you disagree with their suggestions, use that clarity to politely thank them for their suggestions (you asked for it, after all) and then finish by completing your vision on your terms.

THE LAW OF DIMINISHING RETURNS

In every undertaking, there comes a point when the application of additional effort fails to yield proportional results. In other words, you may continue to spend more resources (time, energy, money, thought), but the return on the investment steadily decreases. This isn't just an idea. It's a "law."

The Law of Diminishing Returns is an economic principle that can be traced back to nineteenth-century England. Early economists, including Thomas Malthus and David Ricardo, observed that farmland became less fertile, and therefore less productive, over time. The resources (seed, labor, etc.) it initially took to produce a given crop failed to produce the same results year after year.

This idea has, since its inception, become universally applied to everything from manufacturing to psychology. And, in a chapter all about following through, the same notion serves to bolster our concept of "completion."

When you apply yourself to a worthwhile effort, you may initially struggle as you develop the skills and knowledge to tackle the challenge. Then, as you begin to gain traction, you will notice measurable strides and meaningful results. After encountering setbacks and breakthroughs that vary depending on the size and difficulty of the project, you begin to see the finish line; you sense the impending completion of your journey. When you are "almost done" is when your resolve is most tested, as are the skills and understandings you developed along the way.

Bear down. This is the time to finish the task proudly, by going beyond what was expected. Go to eleven! But there will come a moment when you will sense that the additional effort is no longer yielding meaningful results. You have encountered the Law of Diminishing Returns. This is when you should wrap it up. Resolve the remaining questions and handle the details that need to be handled. But end the effort. You're done. Congratulations!

TIME'S UP!

Time can be a great tool for follow through, especially when deadlines are enforced. When we set and respect due dates, we become increasingly focused on the finish. In chapter 12, I encouraged you to set deadlines and promise completion as a means to lean forward and engage the force of commitment. Here, it is time for you to honor your commitment, engage the forces of focus and determination, and deliver what you promised.

As the deadline approaches, you may find your anxiety building. Stress may take on a new meaning. Don't be debilitated by these factors. Instead, use them to focus on following through. Of course, we cannot avoid instances where our time lines "slip" to a new date. Should this happen, don't view it as a devastating development or failure. Resolve to keep a new, more informed deadline. But if it is possible to finish on time, do so, even if it requires a supreme follow-through effort. The sense of accomplishment you will feel will be multiplied when you can say you got it done on time, as promised.

Upon Completion

As you move forward from this moment in your life, take some comfort in how far you have already traveled. Stay the course. Keep stepping forward. Find the rhythm of your movements, and resist the temptation to sprint to the finish line. Slow, steady, purposeful progress will get you there soon enough.

After all, you will never reach your full potential—it is infinite. Every completion (including this book) marks a new beginning, a chance to increase your commitment and rise to meet another previously unforeseen challenge.

Look up. Lean forward. Embrace the off balance moments. That's what life is all about.